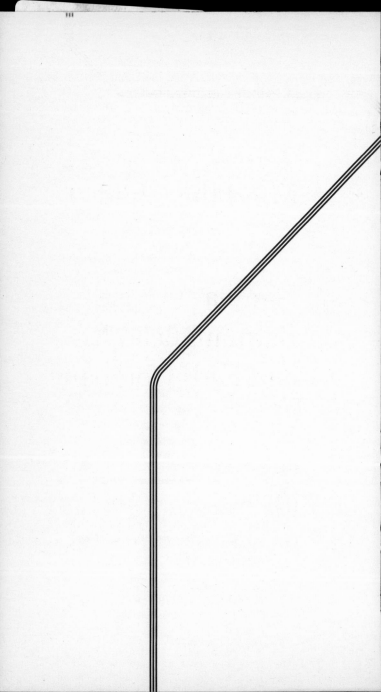

Mind the Child

Camila Batmanghelidjh and Kids Company

PENGUIN BOOKS

PENGUIN BOOKS

Published by the Penguin Group

Penguin Books Ltd, 80 Strand, London WC2R ORL, England

Penguin Group (USA) Inc., 375 Hudson Street, New York, New York 10014, USA

Penguin Group (Canada), 90 Eglinton Avenue East, Suite 700, Toronto, Ontario,
Canada M4P 2Y3 (a division of Pearson Penguin Canada Inc.)

Penguin Ireland, 25 St Stephen's Green, Dublin 2, Ireland (a division of Penguin Books Ltd)

Penguin Group (Australia), 707 Collins Street, Melbourne, Victoria 3008, Australia
(a division of Pearson Australia Group Pty Ltd)

Penguin Books India Pvt Ltd, 11 Community Centre, Panchsheel Park, New Delhi – 110 017, India

Penguin Group (NZ), 67 Apollo Drive, Rosedale, Auckland 0632, New Zealand
(a division of Pearson New Zealand Ltd)

Penguin Books (South Africa) (Pty) Ltd, Block D, Rosebank Office Park, 181 Jan Smuts Avenue,
Parktown North, Gauteng 2193, South Africa

Penguin Books Ltd, Registered Offices: 80 Strand, London WC2R ORL, England

www.penguin.com

First published in Penguin Books 2013

005

Copyright © Keeping Kids Company Limited, 2013
All rights reserved

The moral right of the authors has been asserted

Set in 11.75/15pt Baskerville MT Std
Typeset by Jouve (UK), Milton Keynes
Printed in England by Clays Ltd, St Ives plc

ISBN: 978-1-846-14655-8

www.greenpenguin.co.uk

Contents

*All the art included in this book was
produced by the inspirational young people
who are supported by Kids Company.*

*All royalties from this book go to
Kids Company.*

Camila

I have an ambivalent attitude towards the Underground. I recognize that it serves a lot of people, delivering them to their destinations. But for me, it sadly acquired an alternative fascination. When I was fourteen, my sister jumped in front of a train. Luckily, she fell into a hollow in between the tracks, so although the train did go over her and injured her leg, she survived. I called it 'the thirty-pence suicide attempt' because that was the cost of her ticket, a pink slip of paper that I have kept to this day. I often wonder about the shock the driver must have experienced, and how horrific the event was for him as well as for my sister, who had to be carefully rescued from beneath the train.

Since then, each time someone jumps on the tracks, bringing the station to a halt, I find myself preoccupied with the discrepant journeys we all take in life: the parallel existences of the destination-driven crowd, who move rapidly to complete a life task, and the destination-despondent, who decide that life is no longer worth pursuing.

Subsequently, my sister did commit suicide, but before that, when I was nine years old and living in Iran, I had very clearly decided to take up a commitment to work with disadvantaged children. My own childhood was sheltered, as was my sister's. We had enormous access to opportunities and rich experiences afforded by the wealthy environments we were born to. When I was fourteen and she was twenty-five, our lives turned upside down because of the Iranian revolution. My father, who had made his money legitimately, did not run away, and as one of the most well-known men in Iran he was captured by the revolutionary forces and imprisoned in Evin, the high-security prison. Every day, we lived with the fear and uncertainty that he would be or had been executed. Sometimes pictures of bodies on mortuary tables were sent to us, suggesting that he was among the dead. As communications were ruptured, the fantasy of what might be happening to him drove my sister to her death.

Even though her loss was deeply traumatic, it wasn't personal trauma that compelled me to work with children – it was a love of serving others. I can feel you rolling your eyes, thinking 'What kind of a fruitcake is this?' I recognize that some people may perceive those who want to help as wounded healers, compensating for personal vulnerabilities. However, some of the world's richest cultures put care-giving at the forefront of their agenda, and see it as an expression of refinement rather than failure or weakness.

I had two grandfathers: one was a self-made multi-millionaire by twenty-one, and went on to generate extraordinary personal wealth; the other was financially poor, but dedicated his life to healing children. I recollect people queuing up in the street to bring their children to him for medical treatment. There was something beautiful about him: he was understated and graceful, and I could see something of his spirit hovering a dance in the air, as if compassion was making him high.

I could best be described as an odd child. Having been born very premature (two and a half months early, weighing 1kg), I wasn't put in an incubator because they thought I was going to die anyway, so I think I spent a lot of time in an abstract space between life and death. I recollect being very sensitive to atmospheres, and to people beyond their visible skins. As I travelled in our police-protected car, I used to look out of the window and notice children on the streets selling matchboxes. It wasn't long before I realized the discrepancy between our worlds, and the lack of material possibilities in other children's lives. I started taking food from our house and leaving it outside the doors of poor people so that they could feed their children. I didn't want anyone to know that I had done it, because I didn't want anyone to feel grateful. (The rest of the time I delighted in attempting to fly in our garden, and to this day I am sure that through flapping my arms I did lift off the ground!)

So my preoccupation with children of other lives began very early. My mother bemusedly agreed to provide me with a subscription to a psychological magazine about childhood development, which would arrive every Wednesday. I would hug it and climb into bed with it, determined to read every article from beginning to end. It was as if I was born with an instinct, for which I sought words and definitions. In my twenties I completed a psychotherapy course, and embarked on a career meeting some of the wonderful children whose voices will be heard in this book.

We tend to look at the Tube map only when we have a destination in mind. Take the

Victoria Line: its sky-blue snakes clearly through the tangle of other lines, from Brixton in south London all the way to Walthamstow in the northeast. In this book, I want us to take a less direct route. I want to introduce you to some of the extraordinary kids struggling daily with the dichotomy of living and dying, who I have met over the course of twenty years through my work at Kids Company and, prior to that, through a range of other settings. Kids Company works with tens of thousands of young people each year, and, naturally, only a few of their voices can be heard here. But I hope those who we are about to hear from can show you something of what life is like for hundreds of thousands of other vulnerable young people like them in our nation's capital. These are the children we tend not to see, or, if we do notice them, it is to demonize them. They will be sharing their stories with us throughout this book, boarding and alighting on our journey as fellow passengers. Perhaps we can learn to be more mindful of these children of the underground.

Mind the Gap

There is a sinister drama to the warning 'Mind the gap'. The phrase has been spinning in my head.

The dark gap into which some of the UK's most vulnerable children disappear is not a physical hole, it's a psychological one: the vacuous, absent, thoughtless abyss generated by decision-makers unable to imagine and conceptualize the existence of children living in the underbellies of our cities; invisible citizens of Great Britain who have neither the voice nor the power to hold politicians accountable for the failure to care for them. Action for Children estimate that at least 1.5 million vulnerable children struggle to survive their childhood in the UK,[1] and in 2007 Unicef reported that Britain was at the bottom of the league of 21 wealthiest countries in the world for the wellbeing of children.[2] The gap is big, and is not minded.

Here is a new kind of Underground ad:

THE PERVERSE TRIUMPH

In Britain adults have won. They dominate the decision-making process and the public narrative; they do politics, commission enquiries, distribute grants and decide that children are criminals against whose violations they have to be protected. And here are their achievements:[3]

More children are locked up in Britain than in any European country.[4] More than 80 per cent reoffend within two years.[5] 95 per cent of young offenders have mental health problems.[6]

Britain is among the six richest countries in the world, and yet we have the highest child-poverty rates.[7]

The average age of women when they become involved in prostitution is just twelve years old.[8]

68 per cent of young people who run away are not reported to the police as missing. 1.2 million young people aged fourteen to fifteen run away in a year.[9]

In 2011 there were 615,000 referrals to child protection agencies, but only 49,000 children received a robust child protection plan. Many others were left with inadequate levels of help or none at all.[10]

1 in 15 young people are self-harming, of whom 25,000 required admission to hospital because their injuries were so severe.[11]

1.5 million children every year endure child abuse.[12]

In early 2012 more than 1.6 million young people were on Jobseeker's Allowance.[13]

National statistics present an underestimation of difficulties because they capture narratives about children and young people who have come to the attention of authorities. Children of the underground rarely appear in social care corridors and often are too frightened to disclose the multiple challenges they're facing. So to take you closer to the truth of these figures, I'm sharing with you data that has been captured at Kids Company.

Kids Company was founded in 1996 beneath four railway arches in Camberwell. Since then it has grown to provide a sanctuary and be a source of support for some 36,000 children a year, as of 2011. Some 600 extraordinary staff, 11,000 volunteers and thousands of donors annually work together to make our organization a genuine safety net for the children falling through society's gaps.

Ninety-seven per cent of our kids self-refer, often because they lack a competent and responsible parent, or because they actually live in fear of their supposed carer. For me, what has been striking is how much vulnerable children help each other on the streets. Children of drug addicts often provide each other with food when their parent has spent the household money on substances. They offer each other comfort when alcohol and drug withdrawal drives their parents into uncontrollable rages.

I have always been touched by children bringing other children to our centres. Most recently one of our boys found a teenage girl at the bus stop who was prostituting. He realized she was hungry and he told her about the fantastic food served at Kids Company for lunch and dinner, and later that day they walked through the door of our centre like a brother and sister. The offer of a free meal, with no strings attached, is often the first indication that the agency cares.

Once trust has been established, the child may take us back to their home – if they are living at home. I often enter these homes with dread. I remember walking into one where the kids had squashed cardboard boxes on top of each other instead of mattresses, and pulled rotten curtains over themselves as bedding. I wanted to cry as I saw the drugs paraphernalia mixed in with broken cots, and the baby crawling over concrete because there was no money for a carpet.

In another house the mother had stuffed her used sanitary towels and condoms all the way up the staircase. She and her seven-year-old daughter often wouldn't speak to each other and would write messages on the walls. The child had written 'Why do you hate me so much?' When we walked into the child's room, there was dog excrement all over her bed. She had no toys, no books; she trusted the blank pages of a diary with her feelings more than she could her mum. She wanted a pink bedroom. In the kitchen rat droppings had frozen into the ice of the fridge. I really wanted to be angry with the mother: how could she have a baby and a seven-year-old in this house in such atrocious conditions? The place stank. I wondered if she was a sex worker because of the multiple condoms. My rage was soon paralysed as the mother described having run away from home when she was thirteen because she was sexually abused. The 21-year-old in front of us was a damaged child, unable to parent her own children.

This family lives on a rich street but they inhabit an underground world. Does the teacher know where the seven-year-old lives? Does the baby's health visitor know about the flies crawling in the baby's nappies? Has a social worker visited? Do the neighbours know? Does anyone care?

Some of Kids Company's volunteers become mentors to the children. A lovely senior banker decided to mentor a few of our boys. I will never forget his description of one of the homes he visited. The father, who opened the door to him, had urine all down his front. Our volunteer pretended not to see this and gratefully accepted when he was invited into the sitting room. The place stank of crack and he began to feel really sick, so he went to the toilet to throw up, but the bowl was full of faeces and in a disgusting state. He just couldn't find anywhere to vomit so he had to go outside.

I so admire him for sticking it out, for all those hours he argued with the boys over not pouring sugar on top of their chicken and chips, teaching them how to hold a knife and fork properly. In between major City deals he would call them to make sure they had their sports kits ready for when they all went to play football together. All the boys he mentored are now doing brilliantly.

There are many such memories to treasure: the day one of the major City banks employed one of our boys, or the day one of our girls sat opposite me announcing her first job at a hedge fund. I was so happy for her.

It makes me laugh when I consider what happened soon after the boy who now works in the City first arrived at Kids Company, aged eleven. Some bankers had come to the railway arches where we first started in Camberwell. The children didn't want me to go into a meeting with them because they wanted to play with me. I kept explaining that I had to go into the meeting because I needed to get some money from the bankers. While I was sitting in the room, being grilled about our income and expenditure, I began to smell smoke. I got up to check what was going on and realized that the kids had poured petrol over the teabags I had used to make tea for the bankers and set them alight. They were delighted that the meeting had been interrupted and that I was out, trying to evacuate everyone, but the bankers were furious, and never gave us funding again.

On another occasion the kids stole the bike of the Comic Relief representative. I thought, 'Oh my God, I'm going to lose another grant', so I sent a message down the 'Peckham bush telegraph' to say the bike had to come back. It was duly returned without a wheel. Whenever we have posh visitors I dread it for fear of what the kids might do.

At night, before I go to sleep, a huge variety of people and children whirl round and round in my head. The extraordinary philanthropist who gives us £300,000 and asks not to be mentioned. The old lady who brings her life savings to our door. The man who sends us a thousand yoyos. Or the estate agents who shut their shops one day a year to collect food for Christmas Day, when we receive some 4,000 children for lunch.

Then there are the kids. The thirteen-year-old who hands over his firearm, which our keyworker delivers to the police station. He never wanted it in the first place. The boy who bites his arms because he thinks he's grown feathers, when what he really wants is to be able to fly away from the harm he is enduring every day. The little ten-year-old girl baby-sitting her six-year-old brother alone in the house when their mother's pimp and other drug dealers burst in, savaging the place. The six-year-old who is responsible for her siblings and attempts to shoplift food because her mum is using the household money to support her drug habit. Children who have been raped, children who stuff their shoes into the holes in their bedroom walls, tossing and turning through the night, trying to block out the sound of mice and rats scrabbling around. All these children want is a parent who can function and provide a sense of safety. It's become trendy to blame the parents, and in doing so to somehow excuse the lack of help available to these children, because their 'feckless parents' should be taking care of them. But children don't choose to be born into dysfunctional families, and when one looks closely at these parents' histories, invariably they have endured disturbing childhoods of their own, without love and warmth.

Children who have been abused and/or neglected pay a price. Throughout their lives they struggle to manage the legacy of the harm they have endured. One of the most painful repercussions is a sense of shame generated by humiliation. There is a difference between humiliation and shame.

Humiliation is a catastrophic loss of personal power to which there are witnesses. In the eyes of the onlooker the humiliated individual, condemned to a diminished position, is no longer an equal. Human beings across all social divides are terrified of losing personal worth in the eyes of others. The terror is primitive; it triggers anxieties about being abandoned and discarded by the group, left alone to fend for oneself. At the root of so much desperation is an attempt to regain dignity, to elevate one's 'credit rating'. The protected (individuals who don't have to struggle for survival on a daily basis) do this by seeking to enhance status, whether by going to the right parties, dangling the right designer handbags, dropping the designer children at the right school with the right grades, or having the must-have expensive holiday and birthday party. Unnervingly, human beings commodify themselves, hoping always to be embraced by the group rather than be attacked by it.

Those who come from more challenging home environments face additional difficulties in ensuring an elevated 'credit rating'. Not only are they required to participate in the consumer rat-race, but they also often have to exhibit violent characteristics to generate a reputation for a lethal disposition, and through their behaviour indicate that they are affiliated to a gang even if they are not. This is so that anyone on the street wishing to harm them can be dissuaded from doing so for fear that the revenge from other gang members will be lethal. Imagine being a young person and tattooing a tear on the side of your face to send out the message that you have killed. Whether you took a life or you didn't, the need for such an act in order to buy personal safety is probably one of the saddest indictments of inner-city childhood in Britain.

Once someone has been humiliated, the condescending stare of the onlooker cuts through their flesh, slicing it with a sense of personal failure. Repeated loss of dignity, whether through active harm or passive neglect, results in the internalization of this sense of personal failure. That is when shame wraps its bleak cloak around the heart, making it sink in horror as the discrepancy is highlighted between what the child aspires to be and the lowly level at which they have ended up.

Entire generations of children and young people are carrying the burden of personal shame. In the newspapers they see themselves reflected back as hooligans, monstrosities, scroungers and specimens of failure. Young people believe that 99 per cent of media coverage about them is negative, yet only 1 per cent of them get into trouble. Those who do end up breaking the law have in the vast majority of cases endured chronically unsafe childhoods.

Recent evaluations[14] carried out give you a sense of the scale of the problems faced by the children and young people who turn to us.

> 90 per cent of over-sixteens were not in employment or education at the time of the initial assessment
> 51 per cent had housing problems
> 33 per cent didn't have a bed

- 18 per cent did not own a single pair of underpants
- 55 per cent reported being constantly angry and capable of exploding
- 84 per cent of children and young people arriving at one of our street-level centres are homeless
- 87 per cent suffer from significant emotional difficulties as a result of challenges they face in life

Those who have experienced shame are driven, by the brain, into a hiding space: they avoid eye contact, they seek a disguise, and they assume a lack of benevolence in others because they believe that they are too ugly and defiled to warrant being welcomed and embraced. In hiding under a hoodie, the shamed child actually manifests anxiety, which the general public interprets as predatory. Adults and young people walk past each other, sharing the communal space, each refusing to see the humanity of the other.

Feeling more and more rejected and

frightened, children describe an insidious process whereby initially they use scary 'masks' to fake being tough. The first mask is usually linguistic: using aggressive language, being derogatory about women and minorities or expressing sadism. The next mask is carrying out aggressive acts, initially at the milder end of the spectrum, such as kicking, pushing and getting into fights. These escalate into beatings using weapons, sexual assaults including rape, and witnessing and administrating torture: burning people with lighters or irons, beating them with baseball bats, at times penetrating people with objects. Some of this activity is captured on mobile phones by the protagonists and put on the internet with the intention of acquiring a fearsome reputation. Before long, what started as a mask takes over the young person, and they feel that they completely lose their own identity and become, as they describe it, 'sick', unable to feel tenderness.

It is important to remember that this process starts because a child feels unsafe and overwhelmed by the harm they are enduring. Rather than be humiliated, they hide behind violence. Often the methods they use to harm others have been used on them.

As the public fear the children more, they tend to avoid them or develop antagonistic narratives towards them, calling them 'scum', saying they should be put in gas chambers, asking for their extermination. You might think I am being extreme, but these are all opinions I've heard the public express during radio call-ins, as well as in person. The children fail to make a link between their being feared and the public's rejection of them. For them, extreme violence has become a perverse norm, so they don't see their own behaviour as exceptionally abusive. They therefore have to find an explanation for why the public avoid them so much and fail to care for them or offer a welcome. It is in this context that conspiracy theories develop. The government's inability to imagine challenging childhoods is interpreted by vulnerable young people at street level as a strategy to keep them trapped in the ghettos of Britain and to allow them to kill each other – as if an implosion, removing from the planet the hated children, will lead to the social cleansing that Middle England is often perceived as wanting.

The lack of courtesy some local agencies display towards young people seeking help is contributing to the erosion of humane values. As stressed social work departments, housing offices and job centres feel overwhelmed by demand outweighing resources, they begin to perceive the help-seeker as devouring, and feel a need to defend themselves. Repeated rejections and the use of derogatory language become a daily verbal assault, peeling away layers of dignity and further rupturing community cohesion. When children observe agents of the state unable to sustain the care-contract, they learn the primary social message: fend for yourself, because no one else is going to fend for you. An individualistic survival strategy is conceptualized at a young age, making the framework for living dog-eat-dog – and you best be top dog. The dynamics of power keep fluctuating as the state suppresses and the ghetto rises up in protest. When children have no legitimate powers, they resort to illegitimate means of ensuring their own wellbeing: violence is a common and much-feared weapon. But at the heart of the violent encounter is a plea for personal safety, a beg for dignity, a hope for equality.

The London riots of August 2011 were a manifestation of the social chasm. Unsurprisingly, the initiators of the riots ended up being the same 'children of the underground', children who have endured years of multiple school exclusions, a reliance on school meals due to parental poverty, unaddressed special needs and, if anyone had bothered to ask them, probably sexual and physical abuse. Here are the real statistics beyond the hype, beyond the lowly figures who ended up before our judges.[15]

Of the young people involved:

42 per cent were in receipt of free school meals, compared to a national average of 16 per cent

66 per cent of those appearing in court were classed as having some kind of special educational need, compared to 21 per cent for the national average

More than 33 per cent had been excluded from school in the previous year. This compares with Department for Education records showing 6 per cent exclusions for all Year 11 pupils

When I explain the dynamics of the riots from the position of the young people who spoke to us, I am in no way condoning the violence. I recognize, as do the young people who witnessed the damage, that much unwarranted harm was caused to completely innocent individuals who had worked hard to create their businesses. Communities spent days being terrorized by the lawlessness. There is no justice in feeling terrified and unprotected.

The general public were exposed to this for four days. Vulnerable children are exposed to it throughout their childhoods, with minimal power to contextualize or walk away. When your home becomes the setting for exceptional fear, and you see no intervention to protect you, your world view is profoundly altered.

In the eyes of the young people, what's the point of sustaining an allegiance to a society that doesn't think about their needs? It is true to say that the tax-paying public is funding the education and health provisions that young people receive. But in the eyes of the vulnerable, the social contract has been trampled on. As one young person put it, 'There is no love for us, so we give them hate.'

Repeated regeneration programmes have invested money in cosmetically upgrading buildings, as if a lick of paint will transform the ghetto into a gentrified environment. The regeneration that has been missed is the emotional one; paying attention to children desperate to be seen so that they can be helped. Emotional regeneration is hard to measure but it's a prerequisite to the overall success of a nation. In this age of austerity some £200 billion were spent on the repercussions of the riots. Imagine if that money had been invested in bolstering the care of children who are yearning to be looked after and chosen for love. So many children choose the street as a safer place than home.

The 'Underground Children'

I asked a few of our young people what they
wanted to share with you from their invisible
childhoods, their below-the-ground existences.
Each one of them wanted to contribute – not
out of self-pity or personal narcissism, but
because being with Kids Company has allowed
them to develop a sense of family cohesion,
as they watch each other negotiate personal
trauma and courageously survive it. As a matter
of principle, we have neither guided nor altered
their communications, so that each brings with
it the raw gift of childhood insight. Let me

give you a warning: childhood maltreatment is a lifelong adversity. There are no miracles. Every day children and young people struggle with its dark implications.

I want you to read the young people's narratives so that you get a sense of the accumulated and often devastating challenges they face. A bit later, when you've met our extraordinary kids, I hope to explain the physical, social and psychological price they pay for survival.

Victoria Line

I get on at Brixton, I'm on the run again from the new foster parents, no one will find me on here. I sit looking at people, imagining where they are from and what their houses look like, the woman across from me has a bag that looks like it cost more money than I can ever imagine, she is tap-tapping away on her BlackBerry, her nails are beautiful and painted red and I wonder if she has kids. If she does, I bet she is really nice to them and she probably has presents for them in her bag.

I like being on the tube because no one bothers me and when I'm travelling I forget everything that is going on. It's warm here and sometimes people leave the end of their lunch or they drop a pound on the floor. The next stop is Euston but I won't ever get off there, never again. At Euston men hang around, looking for kids like me, and they invite you to their flats, where they introduce you to their friends, a girl from my kids' home went there and she ended up dead, from heroin, she was fifteen.

I can sit on this tube all day back and forth because no one sees me really, they say there are cameras everywhere but they don't catch me, I'm invisible to them because I'm just another kid, from a bad background and they don't see me, or this weight on my shoulders.

Sylvie

Crazy Ghost

I know what happened in my past, in the terms that people can stomach: domestic violence, neglect, poverty, alcoholic parents and abuse. All these terms wrap things up in a way that means I don't have to talk about how it felt, what it was, the smell, the feeling in my belly, so here goes.

It's late, really late at night and I'm five years old and I'm not yet asleep and I'm really looking forward to my school lunch tomorrow. The door slams in a certain way and I feel like being sick and wetting myself at the same time. I hear him come in, crashing and banging, looking for more drink, and I clutch on to the sides of the mattress, waiting. We don't have too many plates left so this time I only hear a couple smashing, I hear him calling my mother a bitch, a slag, and then I hear her whimper like a small animal. My head whirls and I need the loo but I can't leave the bedroom because if he sees we are awake he will either take us downstairs and play music really loud and make us dance at 4 a.m. or he will give us kitchen towels to mop up the blood, while my mother sits on a chair, broken. I go to the corner of the room and lift up the carpet and pee into the floorboards, I hope no one catches me doing this, I feel ashamed but wetting the bed is much worse.

Some nights we go to a neighbour's house when he beats my mother really bad, she gives us warm bowls of cereal and I feel guilty because I like the food but I don't like why I'm getting it. We sleep huddled in front of a gas fire until we can go home again, my father disappears for days. The police come, but then they go again, I don't understand what the police do because I thought they stopped bad things. When I'm seven we finally leave and go to a hostel, we sleep one mum, two brothers and little me all in one room, the door is really heavy and they say no one knows where we are, and no one can get in. The social worker comes and they say we can all stay together, they don't give any other help. I'm at my third school and I don't like it, I miss the old one. My brother keeps falling asleep at school because we still don't sleep really well, always waiting for that slam of the door. My mother always seems sleepy lately. I find a bottle of vodka under her bed and try it. She goes mental but she called it medicine and said it made her feel better so I just wanted to try a bit. We get re-housed and I start a new school, no one tells me where my father is and I worry all the time that he will come back, but a part of me wants to see him, as long as he is not angry.

Our new estate is crazy, the police are everywhere but they just seem to chase the boys all the time. My mother takes her medicine and we just do what we want. I get really good at nicking scotch eggs for the boys because we don't really have proper meals. The social worker comes again and tells my mother there are 'concerns'. The lady asks us if we are all OK, we say yes all at the same time, she hurries off. I make this new friend at school and I love her so much, when I go to her house for tea her mum looks worried when I say where I live, I never go for tea again, and it makes me sad.

A new man comes round to the house all the time, him and my mother sleep in the same bed and they stay up late with a lot of people having parties. One of the men sends my brother on jobs where he takes parcels all over the city, he gets so much money and we eat pizza and chips with loads of cans of coke. The house smells so bad,

I don't go into the kitchen anymore and you have to step over a lot of rubbish anyway so we just keep the door closed. My mother seems to sleep a lot, sometimes she doesn't come home for days but we just eat crisps and watch TV. I just get on with things, no one seems to check on me, I could skip school if I wanted but mostly I like going, but it's hard when they ask me what I did at the weekend.

One morning there is a massive smash at the front door, I wet myself because I'm still in bed, I think it must be my father, I run round the house trying to find my mother to save her but there are men in mad helmets everywhere and I see the social worker standing at the front door with the clipboard. They are all looking for something and a policeman carries me to the door and the social worker sits me in the car, I can't breathe properly and my clothes are wet. I can't see my family, then I see my brothers go into a different car but they won't let us speak to each other, I feel sick. The neighbours are all looking and then they bring out my mother's friends, they are in handcuffs and the police have a lot of clear bags, I don't understand why they have my brother's rucksack and my teddy! I get out of the car and I try to run but they bring me back and they tell me my mother is not well, and that I need to go to a safe place while she gets better.

I didn't know I would never live with my mother and brothers again at this point. The boys got sent out of the area for 'protection' and I only saw them now and again in a horrible Burger King at a motorway service station.

I'm twelve years old and I've lived with four sets of foster parents but now I'm in a children's home because 'my behaviour can't be managed'. I think these people are full of bullshit, the last set of foster parents made me eat in a different room with the other foster kid while the family and the 'real' children ate big bowls of pasta with a lot of cheese. I feel like I've been hungry since I can remember. It's not like never eating; it's a bit like being in a rush all the time and only eating one bit of your sandwich before a bird craps on it. There are a lot of meetings all the time but it's just a lot of people talking about me, not to me. They sit around shuffling their papers and I notice they never really look at me, I know why, it's because I'm not a normal child. I'm like a ghost that people can only see at certain times. I run around the city with my friends and even when I'm reported missing no one ever sees me, or finds me. The children's home is crazy, a lot of ghosts causing chaos and the human adults panicking and breaking down, the staff change all the time.

I'm thirteen, and I'm not a virgin. I did it with this man who seems a lot older than me but he told me he is eighteen, me and some other girls go in his car and we go to a house where we smoke and drink. They wait around the home, I realize later they want the girls that won't have a mother and father chasing after them, sweeping them up in their arms and looking after them. Social workers only work 9 to 5 Monday to Friday.

The social worker asks me if I am 'safe'. In my head I wonder why they have all been asking me this my whole life. They don't really want to know the truth, they just need to tick 'child safe' on their list on their stupid fucking clipboard. I'm not a little girl anymore, I'm a crazy ghost and no one is going to fuck with me. If I feel like I'm invisible, just like my whole life, it makes things hurt less.

I took fifty paracetamol one night because I'd heard they could kill you and when they pumped my stomach at the hospital I could hear them saying what a silly girl I was, that I was looking for attention, I wasn't, I was looking for a cloud to sit on. They took me to see a lot of different people: doctors, new secure units, and they all scratched their heads wondering what to do with me, and what was wrong. I felt like ripping my heart out of my chest and showing them the diagnosis 'broken heart, from losing parents, brothers and hopes'. No one knows what to do with me, but as I'm fifteen they just want to contain me because in six months I can go into a hostel, because then I'll be a legal adult. I'm quite worried about being sixteen because then they will tell me stuff they can't now, to 'protect me'. My mother found a man and moved away, we're not in touch but I understand because she always said I had my father's eyes and so she probably sees him when she looks at me, so she doesn't look.

At my review meeting when I'm just past sixteen they tell me I'm going 'independent', I find this quite funny – as if I've been in someone's bosom for the last sixteen years with clean sheets, bedtime stories and hot chocolate every night. I get offered a bedsit, but it's back in the old area, where the boys and girls I grew up with live, and I know that if I go and hook up with those people I'll soon be in a house with some pasty white children, hiding behind a door when my husband comes in from the pub. Instead I start sofa-hopping, going from place to place doing temporary work washing dishes and changing sheets in dirty hotels. No one checks up on me from social services and no one tracks me down, I just drift around and as I go into my twenties the strain on my brain begins to be too much. I go for days without sleeping, eating or even stopping for air. I meet a lot of other ghosts under the arches of Vauxhall and we swallow pills and sniff things that give us shiny smiles all night.

I smoke heroin for what I think is the first time and then realize that it's the same smoke an older girl gave me when I was twelve. This is when I realize I have to stay away from the hard stuff. I still manage to work but often quit jobs and move all around the country, I don't feel like I have anything under my feet, I often wonder if I'm actually alive because it feels like I'm living in a blur. I find it so hard to meet people because I don't know how to explain the easy stuff like where I'm from, where I grew up, where my accent is from and what my past is. I like reading and going to see art and I meet nice friends from fairly stable backgrounds and I back off from the drugs and the partying but I feel like I am unravelling.

Then, after not sleeping for days, I wake up in A & E somewhere in London and a gaggle of medics hang round my bed, they tell me I'm ill, I have to go into hospital, I don't have a choice because I'm sectioned. The law has decided after all these years that it needs to keep me safe and in the months that follow I take pill after pill and I sleep and wake up not knowing what will come. They say

I am mentally ill, that I suffer from bipolar disorder, that I am psychotic. I wonder whether I've been that way all my life but now it's just boiled over. I get put into another hostel and the housekeeper advises me to sleep with a chair against the door and my phone under my pillow. One day I read an article in the newspaper about a woman who runs a charity, she speaks of 'lone' children and young people surviving childhood alone and her words resonate with me, I go to see her and we eat lunch and she tells me that she will look after me and my brothers and help me. She looks into my eyes, like really looks, and she doesn't stare away and become uncomfortable. We drink hot chocolate.

In the years since there have been more sections, I've been on wards with dangerous, ill and frightening people and at times I really have wanted to die just like I did for most of my childhood. But Kids Company don't base things on how old a person is, they base things on what most of the parents of my friends at university do: on love, and a relationship. Sometimes you need people there every day, bringing you pyjamas in hospital, ringing you to get up for a doctor's appointment or for a job interview. When you are sectioned in a psychiatric hospital you are isolated and without a strong family. You could go days without seeing anyone. You can't pop out for clean pyjamas and something decent to eat when you're sectioned. Kids Company send visitors every day when young people are in this situation, and it's crucial to getting better, and getting out.

The perception of 'hospital' may be of a caring place where you are looked after when sick, but in a psychiatric hospital this is not the case. They are basically dumping grounds where people in drug-induced states, the depressed and the sometimes dangerous, are kept. I vividly remember a woman transferred from prison who remarked that the conditions in Holloway Prison were much nicer; the food, the beds, the TVs. I thought this was a bit nuts. There were people knocking on my door for money and cigarettes and the ward staff were agency people who seemed to know little about mental health. It really felt like a punishment, and I swore never to go back there, however ill. It feels like you are just going round in circles from system to system and when you are standing on that platform edge seeing the tube come towards you, your options seem very limited and it's hard to hold on.

On the one hand kids in care are parented by the state, but then rather peculiarly this ends at sixteen or eighteen. I don't know many friends that have been totally independent at this age, and even if they were I know their families would still be there for them if they were ill. It's a paradox being told you're mad when you are pretty sure the systems all around you are insane.

I'm at university, and it's a brilliant thing to do, but when you're from a difficult background it can be excruciating; a constant barrage of questions about background, parents' professions, schooling. What do I say? I don't want to make people feel uncomfortable, but their own prejudice makes me sad. When they do find out your past they remark that they never would have guessed! Apart from that it's a bit of jealousy because I'd really like to be like them. I know we all have problems with parents, I'm not naïve; I'd just like my problems to be on a lower level. I still can't totally see a future for myself, but at least I have a base now, somewhere clean which Kids Company painted so simply and beautifully – it wasn't just paint, it's so much more than that. I can feel the weight beneath my feet more these days and with help I'll hopefully finish the degree.

I often wonder why they didn't make us all safe at the beginning, like when we were born. My father didn't suddenly turn into a violent alcoholic when we popped out, he was 'well known'. The social workers say that all children have a right to a family life, preferably with their parents. That's all they say. I spent a long time wondering where my father was, I'd imagine him looking for us drunk and angry, but he wouldn't have been to see me because I was a ghost. When I did find him again there wasn't enough time to sort things out, he died.

Sylvie

Lonely's Story

My brother said I can come to his party, I'm gonna get dressed up, I wish I had a friend to come with

me, but I don't. I'm nearly 12, I should have friends,
I hope I will one day. I'm at my brother's house, it's
just him and his boyfriend, they are drinking, they're
giving me loads of drinks, I love my brother, he's
so cool! They are taking ecstasy, they give me one,
wow it feels crazy! We're all dancing, having a good
time, celebrating New Year.

I feel sick now. I vomited three times, I don't
like the way I feel. My mum won't answer the
phone, she never does. My brother keeps laughing,
then he falls asleep, whenever he falls asleep
it's impossible to wake him up. His boyfriend is
still partying, I think he is high. I feel too sick, I'm
gonna go to sleep in my brother's room because
he's sleeping on the couch. My brother's boyfriend
wakes me up, I'm still half asleep, he puts his
hand over my mouth, I'm scared. I'm screaming my
brother's name, he hits me and starts touching me,
I'm in tears, I'm screaming stop, stop. He put his
thing inside me, it hurts, I'm trying to get away, he's
holding me down. It's over. He lies down, I run to
my brother, try waking him up, even pour water on
his face, nothing works. I'm bleeding, I'm in pain,

I run home, it takes me two hours to run home.
I have a bath, look at my mum and want to tell her,
but I don't think she's in a good mood, I'll just go
to bed. I cry, then go to sleep. I hope I'll forget this
night.

I just got to school, had to walk again because
my mum wasn't up. I hate school, people always
tease me because my clothes are dirty but I don't
know how to wash them, I don't have any money to
buy new ones. They hate my hair and my freckles
too. It really upsets me, they call me weird and ugly,
I think I am too.

I'm at home now, my dad was sleeping on the
floor when I walked in, and my mum keeps hitting
me, I think she's drunk again. She always cries
and then drinks vodka and then hurts me, I think
she's unhappy. My brother is in prison again, I want
to know why but no one tells me anything. I asked
Mum for some dinner, she always tells me to make
it myself because she's busy making my dad's
dinner. I wish I could eat what my dad eats, it looks
so good. I'm having beans on toast, I make it in a
bowl and cut up the bread and mix it in. My dad's

awake now and screaming at Mummy. I can hear her crying, it really upsets me when she cries. My dad punched my mum, she fell, I started screaming and hit my dad telling him I hate him and to leave my mum alone. My mum's face is bleeding. My dad's laughing and tells me to fuck off. I say no, he should leave us alone. He calls me a fat cunt and chases me up to my room and keeps punching me and banging my head against the wall. It really hurts, it always hurts, I'm so scared of my dad, I think he hates me and my mum. I don't think he liked the dinner my mum made him, the plate was smashed and the food was on the floor. I'm gonna have to clean it. I wish I had brothers and sisters around, maybe they would protect me. The house is quiet again. I want to watch telly downstairs. My dad's staring at me, my mum is in the kitchen drinking again. I ask my dad if I can watch something. He says yes, gives me the remote, I put on *EastEnders*, he stands up and hits me hard with the remote. My mum's screaming now, telling him to leave me alone. I run back upstairs, they are fighting again, I put my hands over my ears and sit in my wardrobe. I hope and pray one day things get better.

Lonely

Living on a Bus

It was 3:00 a.m. I was waiting at a bus stop in Harlesden, waiting for a night bus to carry me to sleep. I was sleeping on the buses most nights, waking with the rough shake of the driver and the cold wind of the destination stop.

I had been waiting for nearly an hour and I was freezing, I kept sliding off the bus stop seat – they were designed specifically so people couldn't sleep on them. Out of the darkness I saw a figure emerging. It was getting nearer and seemed to be talking to me. 'Act your age not your shoe size', it said over and over again. As the man got closer I noticed he was holding a metal baseball bat. I realized the danger, but what shocked me most was that I wasn't scared. I wondered when I'd lost my feelings and become so numb. I had thought a moment too long and the bat hit the side of my face with a reality-bringing whack. I hit the back of the bus stop, slid to the floor and started to run. Luckily, despite the size of my legs, I am a very fast runner and have been practising this muscular art at every opportunity – mainly just to stay moving and stop thinking.

I ran into a 24-hour kebab shop and sat on the floor. The kebab man eyed me silently and then tossed me a chip. I looked at him with animal distaste but ate it anyway. After a while I decided it was time to go back outside. I have always felt happier alone at night. My philosophy is that it is safer to go unnoticed.

When I was on the buses, I was always on edge. But not in the way you might think. I was also completely numb and detached. I didn't really care who was near me and who wasn't, or what I looked like, or if my body ached and my tummy rumbled. I still thought about normal things, about what this meant or what that meant or what was in Egypt. I also could quite plainly see the fear the adults had of me – and it made me laugh. How could these big people be so scared of such a small dishevelled being as myself? I had long since lost hope of being helped and almost drew power from my outsider state. This is not to say that it wasn't hard. I dreamt about being found out as the Princess of Transylvania or the daughter of an Australian magician. But as soon as I woke, it was back to the hard concrete reality. I am nothing. No one cares. And that's just life.

My eating habits were pretty irregular and it is only now I look back that I can realize there was a problem there. I, in fact, hardly ate. Because finding food was such a laborious task, which included walking and walking and hoping and hoping. Whenever I did find food, by scrounging through the bins and nervously eating a sandwich, I always felt sick. It's a strange state being at the bottom. There is so much hate around but also so much love. I realized how much I loved the little things like finding something shiny or looking at a tree. But I hated all the men in suits with their shiny shoes and overflowing sandwiches.

Lolula

The Only Way

I first ran away from home aged eight, running from a violent and abusive father. Both physical and mental abuse were a part of everyday life; it was worse when he was drunk, which was the only time I really saw him. I was picked up by the British Transport Police who found me asleep on a tube at Mill Hill. I was to have many run-ins with them in the years to come. They took me home, back to the place I was running from. My hatred for authority started at that moment; in my eyes they were as bad as my father.

I grew up in Peckham, a place riddled with drugs, guns, gangs and violence. This was where it all began. I soon ran into lads of a similar age; although we didn't talk about it we were all having the same problems at home. We had a common bond, and over the years to come our family grew. That's what we were: a family – we looked out for each other, protected each other – isn't that what a family's supposed to do? We spent every day and night together up and down on trains, tubes and buses, no one could harm us; for such young lads we were hard to stop because we stuck together, that was our strength: togetherness and numbers. We were now a gang, a product of the very environment that was part of our society.

When we were hungry we would shoplift, sometimes trying to go unnoticed, other times we would all just pile into the shop, pick up what we wanted and leave – it was a case of steal or go hungry. One of the first times I was arrested was for theft. Me and a friend were in Victoria Train Station one evening; upstairs in the station is Victoria Plaza, where several food outlets are situated, and alongside the restaurants are toilets which at the time cost twenty pence, which you had to put in the machine and enter through the revolving barrier. On this day we noticed the box that contained the money of paying customers wasn't very secure, and with very little effort we prised it open and slid the box out, which to be honest was nearly as big as me. There we were, dipping our hands in, filling up every available pocket with the money; once they were full I noticed that we hadn't even scratched the surface. I wasn't going to leave all that money there, so we carried this huge box across one of the busiest rail stations in the country. That mission landed us both in custody at Ebury Bridge Police Station in Victoria, one of the many police stations in which I would come to know the custody sergeants on first-name terms.

This was a scary time, but I soon learnt the ropes on who and who not to mix with. No one could be trusted on the street – it made me realize the importance of our gang. We would all run away for days, even weeks at a time; we found a bus depot in Stockwell, a good place to hang in the night to get some sleep on one of the many buses that had retired for the night.

My mind raced as a kid, always thinking about the dangers of my environment, trying to stay one step ahead of any potential threat, or having to be quicker than the next to catch the easy pickings of central London. There we were, smoking dope and drinking alcohol we would have stolen earlier in the day. Dope wasn't hard to come by, it was sold over the counter in cafés on the backstreets of South-east London – well, I say backstreets – two of the cafés were on the same road as a Police Station; how they were allowed to do so still puzzles me today. The police would raid in the morning and they would be back open by the afternoon. This shows how much society cares! I mean, if this was in one of the more desirable parts of London they would have closed them down in the blink of an eye. You could say we were the forgotten community. Those cafés still operate today, ruining generation after generation, hey, who cares.

There were some nice people out there. Many times because I looked so young I'd get people coming up to me late at night asking me was I lost, offering me food; they seemed to look sad. Sometimes I used to think when I saw families out together with their suitcases, heading for the airport, laughing and joking: *Why can't that be me?*

There were some real fucked-up dangerous people out there. I remember the toilets on the main concourse at Victoria Station. I went down to the toilet and found myself in a cubicle. Someone in the cubicle next to me was holding a mirror underneath so that they could look at me.

I shouted out to them, pulled my trousers up quick as possible and pulled the cubicle door open. They were gone just like that, in among the crowd to go in search of their next victim.

You are probably reading this thinking, 'Why wasn't this young man at school?' I struggled at school because I ran away from home a lot; school wasn't really an option for me. I did well at my first primary; I went to school, but keeping me occupied was a struggle for the teachers. I should have been assessed for ADHD (attention deficit hyperactivity disorder) but it looked like they did not know anything other than exclusion. For me it would have begged the question: 'What is going on for this child?' With so much pressure and so few resources I doubt this problem has got any better.

It is a shame life did not get easier after this point; it got worse. I was a vulnerable child who craved love and attention. So when a guy came along that showed me love and attention, he took advantage of my vulnerability. I was eleven years old and defenceless; this pitiful character sexually abused me over a year-long period. Once I realized that what was going on was wrong I hated myself even more. It affected me in many ways. I still have nightmares and night terrors; the shame of it all is like carrying the weight of the world on my shoulders. I kept it all secret for many years. It's harmed my mental health, with bouts of depression and anxiety.

Looking back now, all the drugs I used to suppress those shit, nasty and scary feelings have only made my life worse. Once you are addicted you need a constant supply. The only thing I knew was to get money to buy drugs. I wish I could have managed those feelings, that anger and the hatred for mankind, but when you are alone in this world, going through the system, behaving in this manner, they have only one choice: PRISON. I was punished for the way I felt because I couldn't manage those feelings in a good way.

My first experience of prison was a secure unit called Medway, not far from London. Medway was for offenders under the age of fifteen, with boys and girls in separate units. Each unit was named after a castle. The unit I was in was named Hever Castle.

When I arrived, the defences I had learnt running around the streets of London came up; all the anger I had was just under the surface. One wrong word and I would flip out. Was I scared? No, not for one minute. I felt safe, safe in the knowledge that I had a warm bed and hot food to eat.

Hever Unit was made up of ten cells, a communal area and the staff office. You had your own cell with a shower and toilet inside. The window was a meter squared: metal bars covered with clear Perspex. I spent many hours looking out of that window in a daydream, wishing I could break free. I tried to see whether there was any weakness in their attempts to keep me in there. There wasn't. Every room on the unit was occupied.

After I got out, life went on pretty much in the same way: police station after police station, court after court, prison after prison. The drug-taking become more destructive, along with the drug of choice; also came bigger sentences, and an angrier man. I say man – I felt as if I had been on this shithole of what is called Earth for an eternity. I hated the way I felt and looked and the only thing on this Godforsaken planet that could change that feeling was drugs. All of this had taken and was still taking its toll on my mental health, but I was about to get the help I so desperately needed.

I was sent to a psychiatric hospital in London, where I was diagnosed with complex post-traumatic stress disorder. I also suffered from anxiety and obsessional behaviours. I was discharged from the hospital on medication that stabilizes my moods. I am starting a therapy called EMDR (eye-movement desensitization reprocessing therapy), which is a technique used for people who have suffered trauma. I am starting to get some self-worth and self-belief. I have been clean from drinking and drugs for four months. I attend meetings of Alcoholics and Narcotics Anonymous on a daily basis and will continue to do this for the rest of my life. I enjoy writing; I am currently working on a screenplay, hoping that this will educate young people and the powers that be about how they could do things differently.

Matt

A Stop at the Platform

Childhood maltreatment has a lifelong legacy. Low self-esteem and an inability to sustain employment and relationships are the visible components, but with the advances of neuro-imaging technology we're now realizing how much more profound the damage is. The implications are etched into the brain, the physiological and cognitive functioning, neuronal development and even genetic expression.

The science around the consequences of child abuse is rapidly evolving. As I communicate with you, new and more complex findings will emerge, which will change our understanding and hopefully improve our treatment of maltreated individuals. But for the purposes of this book, I want to make the science accessible and, therefore, I'm vastly simplifying the explanations, without, hopefully, compromising their sophistication.

And now, to a simple brain lesson (see Figure 1). We need the front part of the brain, the prefrontal cortex situated just under the skull, to manage the more emotionally driven centres of the brain, situated mid-brain, called the limbic system. The more primitive part of the brain (the brain stem) goes down from the back of the head into the spinal cord. This area is predominantly responsible for regulating our basic requirements related to breathing, heartbeat and so on.[16]

Until recently scientists believed that our genetic programming in effect predetermined the course of our development, and that it was only a matter of us growing up into the

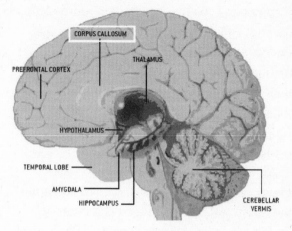

Figure 1. The brain

realization of the predetermined biological framework. However, we are now realizing that, actually, human development is much more complicated than we imagined. In fact, the care conditions that we're exposed to and the quality of the intimate relationships we engage with – starting with the mother-baby dyad – determine a significant component of our development. Human relationships sculpt our brains and set our physiological thermostat.[17]

The brain doesn't develop in one go; its development is from the bottom up and from the back of the head to the front. Therefore, the more primitive parts of the brain, starting with the limbic system, reach full development sooner than the prefrontal cortex. Current research is suggesting that the prefrontal cortex, the part of the brain situated above the eyes, doesn't fully develop until the early thirties,[18] leaving many young people more powerfully driven from their limbic system – the bed of emotionality and memories.

It is not just abuse that harms brain development; witnessing the harm done to others, as for example in cases of domestic violence, or simply being constantly ignored and negated, can cause a cascade of developmental challenges.[19] The repercussions can present as the brain acquiring a diminished efficiency. The unharmed brain processes electrical and chemical messages via the shortest and most efficient routes, whereas the harmed brain, i.e. a brain impacted by abuse, not only develops structural deficiencies (such as a smaller pre-frontal cortex), but also exhibits functional inefficiencies, leading to difficulties with a wide range of so-called 'executive functions', such as working memory, behavioural self-regulation and problem solving and planning.[20] Other parts of the developing brain are also sensitive to the stress caused by childhood maltreatment, leading to abnormal activity in other areas of the brain such as the hippocampus and amygdala (responsible for memory and emotion respectively).

Once one area is damaged, there can be consequences in other areas. That is why harming a developing child is such a public health concern.[21]

Some of the key players in brain functioning are the spaghetti-like structures called neurons. When we're born, billions of these are available in our brains. Some know what to do, others are waiting to be programmed and many are, in fact, surplus and will, over time, atrophy.

The way in which human relationships

sculpt the brain is that as someone interacts with us, especially in the early years of our lives, the quality of that interaction and the requirements of it build information in our brain through strengthening neuronal connections. As the mother coos to the baby, her constant adoration, verbalization, stroking and even disappointing of the child prompts him to repeatedly respond. In the repeated responses, neurons learn different tasks and can be described as developing expertise.[22] The more the neuron is asked to do, the more robust it becomes and its dendrites – the connections at the tip of each neuron, a bit like the branches of a tree – proliferate because they're being used. Those branches that are not used die through lack of use. Brain volume increases as more brain fibre connections are generated. Lack of human care inhibits the development of a child's brain. Equally, toxic stress – prolonged overwhelming, overpowering stress – can atrophy neuronal pathways and alter their density.[23]

Figure 2, below, shows two three-year-old brains. The one on the left belongs to a child who was well looked after, while the child on the right was extremely neglected, experiencing sensory deprivation. Look how much smaller it is, and note the dark cavities in the middle and on the sides. This is lack of brain structure, a consequence of lack of interaction, stimulation and care.[24]

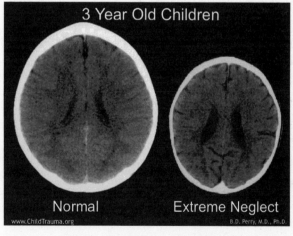

Figure 2. Two three-year-old brains

There has been much talk about the optimum phase of brain development, often referred to as the 'critical period', before the age of three. Although it is true that that is the most rapid phase of infant development, the brain continues to grow and change throughout a human being's lifespan. The continuous neurodevelopment is referred to as neuroplasticity – the brain is a bit like Plasticine; able to be changed by the manipulation of another human being.[25, 26]

Broadly speaking, the first three years are about attachment to significant carers, with the mother being the most crucial carer. By 'mother', I am referring to anyone who functions as the primary carer; this could be a father or a non-related care-giver. From four until ten is the period when peers play a significant part in how an individual evolves, as this is the critical period for social development. During the teenage years, the brain undergoes a massive redevelopment, with the prefrontal cortex of teenagers' brains weakening in capacity as neurons atrophy and reorganize, leaving most teenagers predominantly driven by the emotionally driven centres of their brains, the limbic system.[27] The brain completes its redevelopment phase at the age of approximately thirty, although significant improvements (such as a greater ability to make pro-social decisions and regulate emotions and energy) are noticed from the age of twenty-five in girls and twenty-seven in boys.

From the recovery of some stroke patients, we have evidence that even if areas of the brain are damaged, new networks of connections can be reinitiated through stimulation.[28] Stroke patients who have lost the capacity to use an arm can re-train their brains to regain skills by constantly exercising the arm: our brains are forever evolving, albeit at a slower pace, in our adult lives.

Childhood maltreatment significantly impacts brain development from three perspectives. Firstly, lack of maternal attachment and care is the most significant assault. When you have lacked love and care, the front part of the brain – the prefrontal cortex – doesn't develop properly, literally because the neurons within it haven't been activated by care.[29] So individuals with diminished frontal-lobe capacity struggle to be pro-social; they find it difficult to understand another person's point of view.[30] They are poor at planning and, most significant of all, they don't have sufficient strategies to self-calm and self-soothe. In short, they can't put the brakes on the emotional drivers emanating from the emotional part of the brain. Even without child sexual and physical abuse, the maternally deprived child who has not had good quality care and attachment exhibits unsettled, agitated and anti-social behaviours.[31] In later life, such individuals will struggle to hold down jobs, they will lack consistency and often end up using substances such as drugs and alcohol in an attempt to dampen down and modify their emotional responses. They want relief, they want calm, they seek tranquillity, but their own brains can't provide it for them, so they attempt to achieve it through artificial means.

The challenge is compounded for those who, in addition to poor maternal care, are exposed to physical and sexual abuse, or are witnesses or victims in situations of domestic violence. The chronically frightened child releases vast amounts of fright hormones from the adrenal glands situated on top of their kidneys. As the child stands in the room, not knowing whether he or she will be battered, relentless fright triggers a cascade of chemical activity in the brain, the gut and at cellular levels. In effect, the body is marinated in fright. Adrenaline can propel the individual to either run away (flight), or stay and fight.[32]

Little children have the capacity neither to run away nor to fight. Consequently, in a violent situation they are powerless victims at the receiving end of overwhelming abuse. At this stage, the most they can do is plead with their abuser or attempt to hide in the confined spaces of their homes. Blow after blow, the harm they endure is sealed as a memory in their limbic system. The way such memories are banked is key to the repercussions experienced later. The fright hormone seals the abusive encounter, freezing the details of it: the sweat of the individual battering them, the tone of his voice, the pain of his punch, the suffocation of having the adult body on top of the child's face. Every detail is held rigid, unprocessed, defying time or history. Memories of maltreatment are in the here-and-now, even years later, in the mind of a grown-up.

It is these graphically memorized traumatic events, coupled with the release of the fright hormone, which scientists believe alter the functioning of the emotional parts of maltreated individuals' brains.[33] Research is showing the impact of abuse on the electrical, chemical and structural functioning of children's brains. The pictures in Figure 3 are of two eleven-year-olds' brains.[34] The one on the right belongs to a child who has been maltreated; notice the enlarged ventricles, the

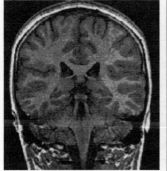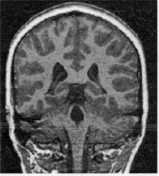

Figure 3. Two eleven-year-old brains

butterfly shape in the middle of the brain, compared to the brain of the eleven-year-old who has not been maltreated.[35]

The challenge of child abuse for the abused individual is not only that the structure and functioning of the brain change, important though this is. The worst part of it is that the abused child in effect constantly operates through two time zones. One is the adult here-and-now being, the other is the harmed-child being. The adult is constantly trying to function in the world, leaving behind the horrific childhood in order to cope. But the harmed child, left unaided and alone, will seek assistance, regurgitating the abusive moment over and over again.

The adult is asleep and, in nightmares, the harmed child inside plays back the old abusive memories. During the day, events in the outside world generate characteristics which unwittingly match the original abuse. It might be a boss shouting at an employee, rekindling the feelings of the harmed child being shouted at by an abusive father.

Three or more characteristics providing parallels to past abuse are sufficient to completely overwhelm the brain by generating neurophysiological distress from the limbic system,[36] and powerful enough to shut down the frontal lobe's rationalizing capacity, leaving a grown individual as emotionally defenceless and victimized as they were as a three-year-old child. Some adults re-experience the abuse memories so potently that they wet themselves, losing bladder control when the heartbeat escalates and the fright hormone revs up in preparation to flee or fight. This is when a grown man will deliver a blow to another as if he were his three-year-old self, propelled by rage and revenge towards his abuser.

One of the first things we learnt about the way to help maltreated children was to listen to the abused individual. Each person absorbs and reacts to interpersonal harm in different ways, but there are common themes which can inform treatment models. Simply put, childhood maltreatment requires a systemic intervention combining psychological, educational and physiological components.

The first port of call is the limbic system: how to calm down the revved-up emotional parts of the brain. The best way to think about it is as a glass too full of fluid. Substitute the liquid for tension and you'll realize that the primary function of a therapeutic worker is to help the maltreated individual manage tension and stress more appropriately.

Some young people try and achieve personal

relief by harming themselves, cutting into the skin or banging their heads into walls, punching windows or pulling hair out. The actions need to cause significant pain as, through the pain, they can evacuate the tension that has built up in the body and mind. These are the 'internalizers', people who don't harm others to achieve relief, but instead harm themselves. Their desire to fight turns inward and can present as a deep and destructive depression, fuelled not by hate for others but hate for the self. Internalizers can go on enduring this violent self-hatred and become so exhausted that they present as lethargic, unwilling to flee or fight. They are in a disconnected, almost catatonic state. When you're with them, you feel powerless and bleak, because their energy has a hopeless deadness about it.

The 'externalizers', on the other hand, attack other people to try and get tension relief. So the primary task of the therapeutic intervention is to achieve limbic system tension relief by more constructive means. At Kids Company we have

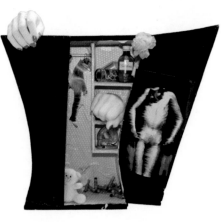

found that our children benefit from intensive physical exercise, to the point of exhaustion, as a substitute for harm caused to the self and others. Team sports aren't so good, because they require the player to think of other people. Those driven by limbic tension are less able to focus on others, so more individual intensive activities like skipping, boxing and running are better.

In order to diminish the power of those potent memories stored in the emotional parts of the brain, they need to be processed carefully. This is where art therapies, play therapy and recounting of experiences come in useful. In effect, the therapist becomes a compassionate companion alongside the child, allowing through sometimes symbolized play the traumatic encounter to be acted out. The child assaulted by the mother might get the mother rabbit to bite the baby rabbit in the sandpit, without owning or explaining that the harmed baby rabbit represents him and the ferocious mother rabbit his mother. The task for a skilled therapist is to help the child define the victimized moment and feel safe enough to experience the emotions that were frozen because he was too frightened to allow the experience of it. At first, the child is given the opportunity to react through the baby rabbit play and then, perhaps, the behaviour of the mother rabbit can be explained, rationalized. In the process, the child who was at the receiving end of the harmful experience acquires, through play, some mastery over their trauma.

A range of trauma-recovery programmes, including eye-movement desensitization and reprocessing (EMDR) and more conventional therapies, work along exactly the same principles of compassionately revisiting the stored memories, allowing a recounting, a reaction and a re-assimilation of them, with the therapeutic worker as the moderator so that the recounting doesn't lead to re-traumatizing. On a more humanitarian level, the child is told that this should never have happened to them,

and that they did not deserve to be harmed
in this way. A sense of moral outrage helps
restore dignity to a young person who has been
catastrophically denied it.

Parallel to dealing with limbic system
deregulation, there is a need to develop the
individual's personal capacities to manage the
repercussions of childhood maltreatment. This
is where attachment between a therapeutic
worker and a client becomes so important.
In providing a caring response the therapist is
helping to develop neuronal pathways in the
frontal lobe through which the ability to self-
care is enhanced. The field of trauma recovery
is evolving. We now understand that, while the
mind stores and processes abusive encounters,
the body undergoes a parallel process
without holding the story of the abuse but
nevertheless retaining its physical impact. So
body treatments such as massage, reflexology,
osteopathy and Reiki become hugely important
to the release of tensions within the cells,
and to programming into them the notion of

tranquillity often missed by individuals who, throughout their childhoods, have lived through chronic terror.

Some traumatized individuals report finding rhythmic activity to be very helpful. This can include drumming, spitting lyrics (rapping), listening to music and deep breathing exercises – in fact, research on monks who have been meditating demonstrates that meditation and deep breathing can help regulate activity in the limbic system.

A similar principle is used by people who practise mindfulness. The idea is that the individual develops the capacity to sit comfortably and almost watch himself having an emotional reaction, rather than engage intensively with the emotional reaction. The further outside the dramatic experience, the more the individual is thought to be able to look in as a calm observer and make appropriate decisions.

Individuals who have been harmed report losing the ability to think calmly about what is happening to them. The tornado of their own emotional reactions overwhelms all their pro-social strategies and swallows them into the frenzy.

Therapeutic work with maltreated individuals is a long and complex process, because abuse delivers attacks on the whole fabric of a human being. The truth is, people don't recover from childhood maltreatment – they learn to manage it.

From Underdog to Top Dog: Attempts to Survive

Not all children who have been maltreated go on to harm others, but there will always be a self-destructive price to pay. Sometimes the very abuse that has been endured is adopted as a way of being. It's almost as if, in choosing to inflict the bad experience on oneself or on others, one is still better off than being powerlessly exposed to it.

The unconscious resolve of most maltreated children is to acquire some form of mastery over their trauma. Having been a victim, they make a vow to themselves never again to be victimized by another. Perversely, this can present itself as the abused individual taking charge in an abusive encounter. For example, a sexually abused girl might begin working as a prostitute so that, rather than having to endure the sexual desire of predatory men powerlessly, she is actively soliciting it, thereby retaining a sense of control over the situation.

Other sufferers may develop the compulsion to repeat the abusive encounter, this time adopting the perpetrator's position rather than the victim's, because actively doing something bad to others is better than passively having something bad done to the self. It is striking how many perpetrators' abusive behaviours mimic the characteristics of the abuse they have encountered themselves.

Disturbances can develop in those who have been significantly harmed. They may experience envy towards people who have not been abused, and wish to abuse them so that there can be an equality in being mutually harmed. Sometimes people who have been abused try and control their negative thoughts and feelings by developing rituals which have an obsessive-compulsive nature to them. These can be rituals to distract or compulsions to clean, because the individual feels preoccupied and dirtied by the abuse.

It is very important to distinguish the moral argument from the psychological one: however repugnant the behaviour exhibited by abusers might be, it needs to be understood in the context of personal harm experienced. Strategies to prohibit the acting out of harmful behaviour are important for maintaining social order, but sanctions and punishment don't lead to recovery. In order to achieve genuine reparation, even the most vilely behaved human being requires tenderness and compassion.

A young person at Kids Company describes the poignant journey to child prostitution:

Children of the Night

The lights indicate and flicker in your face, you instantly come alive and step out of the shadows. It's the best feeling of achievement in the world! You're being called to the stage and rewarded for your talents.

Sadly, this is not your university graduation ceremony, there are no gowns and hats, loud applause or proud parents crying. You're not even of university age, you barely have pubic hair at age thirteen. That's the age I started . . .

It's the backstreets of a rundown industrial estate. The floor is decorated with used orange-top syringes and the graffitied walls are illuminated by the fading blood-orange sunset in the sky. This is the best time on 'the block' because the night is when you feel safest and not exposed. It's like your own little world. I love it when new people who came to work on my block would stare in admiration and say: 'You're gorgeous, I can tell you make a lotta money out here.' It's like a high, wearing these nice clothes and getting all the respect. Car after car cruises constantly around, African taxi drivers, English men in nice cars and the Pakistani and Middle Eastern men in hats and beards. Some look nervous or aroused, they all want the same thing. You give them eye contact and you've caught your prey.

The car edges to the kerb, you give him your friendliest smile, you first look in his face: is he an undercover police officer? Ask him to touch you. Does he look crazy? Look in his eyes to see if he's normal, check the back seats to see if there is rubbish, or is it clean? Is there anybody hiding in the back? You name your price, get in and make sure you're paid first.

I have to take all these precautions because I got into a car and got hit with a belt. A girl who was my friend got pushed out of a moving car and clung on and was dragged up the road; the skin was scraped off her leg down to the bone. It didn't bother us, we just blanked it all out and worked the next night.

Before the Ipswich Murders and London winning the Olympic bid in 2005, the police turned a blind eye to street work so you could be 'on the block' with your friends and not be moved on. My favourite areas were Soho, Earls Court and Edgware Road, because it was built up and lively. The worst areas were the industrial areas in Seven Sisters, Tottenham. A 'street family' of other kids was fun but money changes things, most of the boys and women I worked alongside were either white or black British, I was neither, so when clients see something exotic or different, you become in demand and it's the quickest way to lose a best friend.

The reality hits when you can smell the clients' sweat, their last meal, or see their baby seat and child's toys in the back seat of the car. Some like to be pissed on and drink it, others want you to call them 'dad' and act really young. Most like the 'normal' thing and maybe conversation. All you want them to do is hurry up. I could be in a steamy car, or in an alleyway in Soho, or a damp hotel in King's Cross and I always think and do the same thing. I look up at the ceiling, leave my body and switch off.

When I'm lying under them naked and my legs are spread and they are about to orgasm and cum, for some reason I see in my head the day I was born as a naked baby and the nurses picked me up and handed me to my mother – did they know that the naked screaming baby would one day sell its same body? I think maybe if I were given away as that same baby, I wouldn't have been exposed to things that led me down my path. Not that I blame my family, they did their best with what they knew.

I guess they were as helpless as I was. Seeing your mother getting her head smashed inside the toilet bowl repeatedly by her boyfriend and seeing other females in your family getting bottled, their skulls cracked and bleeding, means you don't feel safe and that stays with you. Just like people kicking your door down in the night and throwing your family members down the stairs or your mother always being drunk or hearing her scream with withdrawal and watching your grandmother crying and begging. Aged seven you feel it's your fault that they love substances more than you. 'I promise I'm going to get better for you, I promise.' Hearing them lie to you turns your heart cold. But no matter how cold your heart is, seeing your mum with no teeth, black eyes and locked up in prison or sleeping in crack houses, that's still my mum – society just doesn't understand she's sick. She's like a little girl and I'm her mum, I will protect her forever. I was only eight and she was fighting with another woman in the street, it was really violent and the woman was biting her hand so I ran out and started hitting the other woman with a stick. I'm really calm these days, but if anybody troubles my mum in her hostel or rehab centre I can switch.

I guess I've been so protective of my mum and family that I don't even tell them the secrets I've had since I was three. Other adults see you're not safe and know nobody will notice or care what happens. They do painful and dirty things to your private parts that change you forever. 'This is our secret, I love you.' It's your dad's brother and other men and it confuses you that this person is meant to care but frightens you into not speaking. I still love him because he would give me clothes, food and make me feel special and I remember the good times.

What's really fucked up is when you grow up you can't have sex or relationships unless there's material reward involved because if there isn't you might feel used and it leaves you powerless and vulnerable like you're age three and eleven again.

As you get older things get worse, not better. It's easier to run away than be thrown out or abused. The police pick you up and the social services get involved. You can't trust them because they interview you at home and your carer is listening through the door; you know because you can hear their footsteps and heavy breathing outside. If I told the truth things could get worse.

The worst thing is your belly hurting for food and no amount of crying will feed you. The best thing is knowing you'll never go hungry again or no adult can reject you and put you on the streets and I think that's why prostitution becomes an addiction. I felt powerful not depending on family members or the social services. You get a new sort of respect from family members and are made to feel important being able to buy everyone clothes and food, but as a teenager all you want is for them to love you and not encourage you. You form a family with other kids in your situation; you support each other whether it's finding out they have been infected with HIV or chasing away older women or boys that try and exploit us. When we are judged by society, it's funny because powerful judges, bankers and off-duty police officers want the most depraved services.

Independence is short-lived for kids in prostitution; 'father figures' lurk in the shadows always. He bought me flowers, we went everywhere in his nice car and he was tall, strong, and made me feel like I belonged somewhere safe. I was sixteen then and he was thirty-five. I didn't tell him I was a prostitute on the street, he didn't need to know. I thought I was streetwise and didn't see what was happening. He always spoke of the future, a family and us having our own business but he said he couldn't think about the future because he owed a lot of money and bad things were going to happen to him if he didn't pay up.

So I went out that day and came back with £200. He didn't ask where I got it from but said I was his 'superstar'. I felt amazing. He later said that the day he met me he knew I was a prostitute but loved

me and didn't care and wanted to marry me – I
never knew that this was his cunning plan and that
he was a pimp on the run for stabbing another
young prostitute in the stomach. Pimps slowly
isolate you from everybody, you're programmed
to just make money. I would come in during the
day and the first thing he would do is search my
pockets and then pull down my underwear and
examine if I had been penetrated or I was hiding
anything. The worst is when they ration your food
or take it away. It's like your body is not yours.
The only benefit I remember of having a pimp or
boyfriend that takes your earnings is when I was
bottled on the head in Peckham, South London and
he came and punished the man. Every day he'd
ask for more and more money. He began arranging
clients for me over the phone and then would drive
and drop me off everywhere around London, from
big hotels in Mayfair to council blocks in Brixton.
When a client tells you his friend recommended
him to see me after fucking me last week, you
feel like you're not a human anymore. The worst
places were the crack houses that made your feet

stick to the carpet and the beds full of faeces. I started to smoke crack cocaine and brown because I couldn't calm down, I'm lucky because it was never a habit for me. Looking back, I don't know why I was in these situations. I decided I wanted to be free of this guy – he smashed a mirror and held it to his neck and threatened to kill himself if I left him; seeing him do that made me feel guilty and I wanted to take care of him and mother him. He said I was the best thing that ever happened to him and his dad used to beat his mum and that's why he said he couldn't stop himself. He recruited five more prostitutes and was sleeping with them, I felt jealous and hurt and realized I was 'washed up', so I began 'putting in work' (cross-country drug couriering) for a man I knew. I think I got into the drug game because I wanted a security blanket for myself, I began to finally put me first, I learnt where to hide the money. It's sad that I saw easy money as a quick option but not education.

I tried to get into education and normal society but he'd say I didn't need school and he stamped on my laptop and made me stay in the house in just my underwear. The more I wanted to lead a normal life and be a child again the harder he'd stamp on my head. I'd scream, 'Please don't hurt me, I love you. Please don't hurt me, I love you', but that didn't stop him stamping till my jaw popped. If he loved me he wouldn't lock me out until I'd made enough money; he wouldn't drag me out of bed and whip me with bamboo canes and belts. 'You're nothing, you selfish bitch,' he'd rage. These pimps are smart bastards: they know not to mark your face as it means you get no clients.

I remember the day when the police raided the house and I was finally free. It makes me want to cry how Kids Company have helped me live again and help myself. It was hard to trust. I owe my life to them and I finally belong. It's scary that so many youngsters are and will be in my situation; I guess I'm just lucky, but why should the lives of innocent, hungry and neglected kids be down to luck? Kids Company tackle this at street level where we actually are.

Me and many of my peers trust Kids Company because they'll never sell us down the river, from a mile away we spot those devoid of altruistic intentions. I've come across organizations that will sensationally expose youngsters' stories in the media or government board rooms without their permission, all for the sake of extra funding. I know times are hard but to exploit kids and leave them with no aftercare or consideration is dangerous.

We are told we can trust smiling charitable adults in civil society, but the politics and ulterior motives I've seen remind me of the underworld. Kids Company genuinely cares. Who else would we have on Christmas day? Dentist appointments? When you've tried to kill yourself and it's failed? I'm alive today because of them.

I wouldn't be half the person I am today if it wasn't for Kids Company staff – Camila, Dannyella, Yolande. Also, Michelle at the SWISH sex workers' project King's Cross. Thank you.

Unlike the start of this story, I will have a graduation ceremony from university; once I finish university I'm going to emigrate far, far away and start again where nobody knows me. I will help all the powerless people everywhere, people that feel too ugly, too fat, unloved, those with no purpose; I'll remind them how special and unique they are. I will be married and have four children with a house and back garden. Maybe I want kids so when I look at them I'm no longer reminded of when I was a child; I'll look in their eyes and see how safe and loved they feel. It's been my goal since age 6.

Angel

The injury caused by perversions of care, the rupture of significant intimate relationships: these are the foundations of personal disturbance. But how these disturbances go on to be expressed is also driven by environmental and social factors. In neighbourhoods where the drug economy substitutes meagre benefits, perversions can be acted out along a spectrum. The individuals who have experienced childhood maltreatment participate in the drug trade, but within it they go on to brutalize others as they've been brutalized themselves.

Those who haven't been sexually abused or physically harmed function at the milder end, wheeling and dealing, engaging in violence as a protection but not going on to perverted behaviours. The risk, however, is that as perversions are acted out in large numbers they lose the power to shock, which lowers the social and moral framework of an entire community. Continual violence and drug dealing can become too normal.

Here is a young person's attempt to acquire mastery over his life, driven by the available solutions within his neighbourhood:

Turning Point

My dad hasn't been around for years and my mum can't deal with me (I think she hates me because I remind her of my dad), so she wants me out the house. I'm seventeen and have little experience dealing with the real world but, fuck it, that's just the way the cookie crumbles. Packed up my little belongings, threw her key on the floor and off I went into the real world. On my way to Bournemouth Road, Peckham, on this cold November morning with two black bags and a rucksack and I was sweating. I reach the centre about 11.30 a.m. and there's about a hundred people waiting to be seen. The atmosphere in here is horrible and dire (people with four plus kids and their whole life on the floor in bags) but I feel kind of good knowing that I'm not the only one in this boat. I waited four and a half hours to be seen by this bitch, only to be told I need a letter as proof I have been thrown out (like my grit to wait this long and my bags weren't enough) and need to come back another day. Pissed off, I leave and ring my good friend who allows me to stay at his house. After a week of this back and forth they finally give me a temporary hostel.

Not knowing where the hell this place is I use my last 20 quid to get a cab there. I arrive outside a lairy pub and the cab man says, 'It's above the pub, mate.' Inside, the stench is unbearable, with about fifty flies in there with me. I think to myself, 'Beggars can't be choosers.' So I try to settle in and make something out of nothing. Two weeks later I return to the housing office and they tell me I have to move to Elephant and Castle.

Luckily my friend had a car this time so he helped me with my move. This place was a lot bigger and it smelt miles better too. It had a little fridge and a stove and I even had a shower in my room. I thought to myself that things were looking up. After a quick trip to the post office to draw my 90 quid and a trip to the supermarket (30 quid on food shopping) I was enjoying my own space for the first time. I even collected my games console and TV from my friend's house.

On the second week of solo living, loneliness was setting in and money was damn near obsolete and I had a call from a friend that there was a party going on and he wanted me to come, and I was at my wits' end so that offer couldn't have come at a better time. After meeting up and trying my best to look half-presentable we headed to Tulse Hill for this house party. 1.30 a.m. came and the party was live and everyone was having a good time including me (after drinking away all my worries).

Then news came that some Brixton boys (gang members) had just turned up and crashed the party. Obviously I'm worried but I can't show it (if you show weakness, you can die from it on the street), so me and my friend manoeuvre closer to the front door just in case. After about forty minutes of everyone feeling on edge the four boys come near to where we are and one of them catches eyes with my friend and they start to do the typical 'staring' routine.

The boy and his dons come over and say, 'Wat are you cool fam?' in an abrupt tone and my friend replies, 'Yea I'm bless fam . . . Are you?' in a confident tone. The boy moves quickly on to say, 'What ends are you from?' and my friend says, 'Nam' (Peckham), and the other guy's eyes widen. Before another word can be said I duck a flying bottle but get a half-decent kick to the face. Testosterone is running high so I shake that off and rise up and land a sweet uppercut on the guy's chin. He goes down and I say to my friend, 'Come we cut real quick'(let's go now); me and my friend go sharply through the front door and run scattily down the hill, trying to get away from the three boys in pursuit. After a few lefts and rights I'm lost but I've evaded the other guy pursuing me. I don't really know what happened to my friend so I look for my phone but I can't find it; nor can I find my money or travel card. Pissed off, angry and edgy, I make the long gruelling walk to Elephant and Castle. I arrive at my front door and walk in, relieved I've made it home because all I want to do is sleep. As I approach my actual room door I see that it's already open. I stand there for about twenty seconds as every scenario plays out in my head as to what I will find in there. I burst in to find it completely empty. It takes me a while to realize what's really gone on and I start to become ablaze with feelings of rage, self-pity and sadness that this could happen to me. My TV, my games console, my cutlery, my clothes, even my bed covers are gone.

I was so pissed I punched the wall and just sat on the bed for about forty-five minutes and then I saw a head pop round my door. It was the housekeeper for the hostel; he asked me if I was OK because I'd left my door open. I replied to him,

'Do I look fucking OK? All my shit's gone.' He said, 'Don't touch anything. I think we should call the police.' Not being a fan of police, I said, 'Call them for what? They ain't gonna do nothing', but he insisted, saying it's hostel policy. They were called about 3.30 a.m. and didn't arrive till 6.00 a.m., so I was even more pissed when they started asking me stupid questions like did anything get taken. An hour later and after all their procedures, the police left saying that they would keep in contact and let me know how the investigation was progressing. (That translates to 'We can't help you, so here is a crime number.')

When I woke up I forgot about my ordeal until I went to turn the TV on and then reality set back in, and to make things worse the 20 quid that I'd put away in a pair of shorts was also gone. So now I had nothing: no phone, no money, no TV – the room reminded me of the inside of a police station detention cell.

I still hadn't heard from my friend so I went to his house, sneaking on the back door of the 36 bus because I had no money. When I arrived he

asked me what happened to me and I explained
my whole drama to him. He was pissed for me
and said I should 'jump on his wave'(i.e. do what
he was doing). My friend was a bit older than me
and he was a drug dealer; he had nice things and
was always able to buy the things he wanted. I was
slightly envious but I felt my path was a different
one from drug dealing. He used to always ask me
if I wanted to do business with him and I would
always decline, but this time I felt as if my back
was in a corner.

As the evening went on and a few spliffs later (I
didn't smoke weed but I needed a release) I asked
him how would it work if me and him went into
business and he said, 'It's simple: I buy the weed,
I get the calls and you deliver it. We split the profit
fifty-fifty.' I said to him, 'When can you put me on?'
and as he started to reply his phone rang. After a
ten-second phone call he said, 'You can start right
now.' He gave me a bag of weed and said, 'Go to
the bottom of the road and link a man in a black
Corsa. He wants a 20 bit', so I went and came back
and gave him the money and he gave me ten quid.

I was shocked to see how easy it was. I started thinking about how quick I could replace my goods that were stolen. He said to come and see him tomorrow and we would sort things out properly. On my way home I was looking forward to the prospect of making some real money for the first time in my life. I finally didn't need to beg anyone for anything or any help.

Two weeks later and loads of bags of weed sold, I felt good. I'd replaced my TV, games console and some of my clothes and I hadn't asked anyone for anything – I had made all the money myself.

Even though I was making money now, something didn't feel right. I felt as if I was selling myself short, almost robbing myself of a decent future and being condemned to a life of drugs and crime that I'd tried so hard to shy away from. One evening, after long contemplation and a few discussions and arguments with my friend, I told him that I didn't want to sell weed anymore and that I wanted to go to college to study and hopefully go on to uni. Even though it didn't sit well with him, he understood.

Well into summer and September round the corner, I went to a few college open days and decided which college I wanted to go to. I brought all the necessary paperwork to sign up, chose the course I wanted to do and a few hours later I had my place sorted on the course for September.

On the first day of college I was raring to go and a few hours in I was already loving my course (I chose a computer course) as they were going through the syllabus. Even though the money I was getting now wasn't even close to what I was getting before, I was content knowing that if I got through this I could at least get a half-decent job, or I had the option of going to university and getting an even better job.

A few weeks into my course (and still loving it) I had a routine Job Centre appointment. I sat down with the adviser lady who quizzed me about my latest job search. I explained to her that I'd just started a college course and I was looking for a part-time position so I could accommodate my college course.

Big mistake. She replied by telling me that if I was not seeking full-time work then I was not eligible to be on Jobseeker's Allowance. So basically that meant my only option was to get a dead-end job now. I was so pissed off and frustrated, but she said I needed to quit my course and start looking for a full-time job. Obviously I wanted to tell her to kiss my ass but realistically when I weighed up the situation I was at a great disadvantage: my rent would be two hundred pounds a week at least, I would need money to survive and I would need to find time for college. After weighing up my options I said to the woman I would go to college next week and withdraw from the course.

As I had a day plus the weekend to return to the Job Centre and confirm I'd withdrawn from the course, I said to myself that I needed to step up the rate of looking for a part-time job as that was the only option I could see for getting out of this irritating situation. Over the three days I think I went to at least two hundred shops handing out CVs and asking for jobs. After all that work I only had three replies but I stayed optimistic. The interview was on Wednesday so I went to the Job Centre with the good news.

The woman asked me if I'd withdrawn from the course and I asked her why. She said if I didn't then she would cancel my claim. I asked her to give me a week to withdraw and at the end of the conversation she reluctantly agreed.

After going to the interview and not getting the job and after exhausting all my avenues I reluctantly gave up my course, went back to the hostel and became a recluse for a few months, only coming out to buy weed to smoke and food.

I got to a stage where I was feeling like the only person in the world. On top of everything else I got a letter through the door saying I owed 300 quid on rent arrears. After much deliberation and soul-searching I came to the conclusion that selling weed was the only option I had of making money.

After a quick reconciliation with my friend and a few long chats I'm in it for the long haul this time. Every day I'm out from 10 a.m. and back in gone midnight; sometimes I don't even go home, I just doss at a mate's until the morning.

Money was being made and my outgoing bubbly self was returning. All the girls wanted to know me but I didn't have time for none of that. My aspirations turned from wanting to become a network engineer to watching gangster films like *Scarface* and *Menace II Society* and thinking, 'One day that's gonna be me.'

Nameless

Thirsting for a Safe Family

Children get dragged into gang life via different routes. Society comforts itself that robust sanctions will stop young people from joining gangs. However, for children whose care conditions are profoundly adverse, prison is described as a welcome respite. As one boy put it, 'In prison I get to sleep on a bed and not on the floor. I get to have regular meals and not be hungry. I get an education, watch films, have a routine and know that someone is taking care of me, even if it's a screw.'

The terror children are exposed to in gang settings is relentless. They are surrounded by stories of people who have been harmed and who do the harming. Whole estates can be under the control of a particular gang, with postcode wars stopping young people from going to another area for fear that they might be attacked. Constant fear can reach a crescendo: threatened children can experience dramatically escalated heartbeats and, as the fear increases, lose control of their bladder and then eventually, at the point of extreme fear, defecate. Dogs are used as weapons, often treated savagely so that they will bite their victims with ferocious force. Firearms are also widely available. They can be rented and returned to the owner; if a firearm is used in an offence its price goes up. Children describe firearms being made available to them by corrupt professionals such as police and army personnel. They also describe large numbers of firearms coming into the country from abroad.

What is very evident is that gangs have a very hierarchical structure. Those making the money at the top can present as very legitimate, sometimes living in expensive houses on the outskirts of London, but they are in fact running a group of young adults, who then run youths, who then run younger children. There are clear rules, boundaries and protocols alongside devastating levels of risk. Revenge plays an important part in gang members' lives. They have to avenge harm done to their team members; thus, one violent act usually results in another. In the process of revenge, completely innocent people can be harmed simply by virtue of the fact that they belong to the same neighbourhood, or postcode, as the perpetrator of the initial act of violence. The system ensures its sustainability by not only controlling gang members through terror but also controlling their immediate family. A young person who is not obeying the rules can be punished via his sister, girlfriend or mother. This can involve rape, petrol-bombing, shooting or kidnapping.

Recent independent research carried out at Kids Company demonstrated that one in

five of our children had been shot at and/
or stabbed, with one in four having had
their immediate family members harmed
in a similar way. The ghettos in which these
children operate are referred to as 'the hood',
short for 'neighbourhood', and the young
people involved are referred to as 'soldiers'.
In 2012 University College London completed
a piece of research demonstrating that the
neuronal pathways of children who had
endured maltreatment resembled the pathways
found in soldiers suffering from post-traumatic
stress disorder.[37] Soldiers are adults, and they
are trained and supported; children who are
being maltreated not only lack support, but
they are described in derogatory ways once
disturbed behaviours, resulting from abuse,
manifest themselves. It is very telling that some
young people choose politically aware names
for their gangs – a notorious gang in Brixton
is called 'Poverty-driven Children'; another is
referred to as 'The Gas Gang', inspired by the
gas chambers of the Holocaust. Peckham is

shortened to 'Nam' in recognition, some say, of Vietnam.

Drug dealers actively strategize the expansion of their business, setting up crack houses in the countryside and making children from London work in them. There are brothels in Luton in which vulnerable young London girls are forced into prostitution. Cannabis fields are now predominantly found in the countryside, so the problem of ghetto violence is potentially spreading more widely into areas where the police force is least experienced to cope with it.

In the narrative below, a former gang leader describes the subtle transformation of innocent children into individuals with a great capacity for harm.

Hood Story

This story is loosely based on one of my childhood peers, whose name will not be stated. In this piece the character's name will be Justin.

Justin from the age of ten was a very sporty child with ambitions to be an athlete. PE was his favourite lesson and most of his peers and teachers acknowledged that he was definitely gifted and had high hopes for him. He lived at home with his mum and brother in a council flat in Brixton; his dad had left the house a couple days before his ninth birthday. Since he could remember, his mum and dad were at constant loggerheads and at least once a month an argument between them would result in his mum being hit. His mum had no one she could really confide in so she told him and his brother all the problems that had been happening between her and their dad, including their father's infidelity and sexual promiscuity.

His first year in secondary school was relatively normal but it did introduce him to the gang culture: he would witness fights between kids in the older years, see some smoking weed in the toilets, and he quickly woke up to the underground hierarchy. Travelling from Brixton to Tooting on the bus, he would come across kids in local gangs. Every day going to school and even in school he would feel intimidated; his close friends shared this feeling. All of them came from council estates; none of them were active in gangs but one of their older brothers was a key player in a notorious gang in Brixton.

During the summer holidays they would all meet up and go to the park to play football and bike ride a lot. One day, en route, they bumped into a group of youths who approached them and robbed their bikes. Even after they had given over their bikes without resistance, one of the kids punched Justin and one of his friends in the face. It really bothered Justin how three boys their age could rob six of them. He stewed over this and rage began to fill his heart.

When Justin and his friends met up the next day they all made a vow that they wouldn't allow this to happen to them again: next time they would fight. They began to congregate at the house of the friend whose older brother was an active gang member; just being in the house and seeing him and his friends coming in made Justin feel better. They all studied and watched him and his friends and on occasion would get a glimpse of offensive weapons and drugs; this intrigued every single one of them.

Justin's brother was in the year below him; his name was Martin. They loved each other as brothers do but also argued as brothers do. Justin and Martin were very different: Martin was quieter, reserved, and would rather spend time on the PC than outside. About two months after school had started Martin's phone was stolen by a boy from the Tooting area; he was an active member of a gang and his street name was Crow. This upset Justin's mum a great deal: they weren't in the best financial position and couldn't afford to replace it – since their dad left the house, money had been very tight. Interaction with their dad had decreased, and he didn't know Martin or Justin had been robbed.

Justin felt he had to make a stark decision. He weighed up the likelihood of this happening to his brother again as very high, so he made an inward decision that he would become a force to be reckoned with. That weekend he went to Anton's house – the friend whose older brother was an active gang member in Brixton – with the secret agenda of asking him for help. He was almost too scared to ask, but then an opportunity presented itself: Anton's brother began a conversation with him, saying, 'I overheard my little brother talking to you on the phone about your brother's phone getting robbed.'

Anton's brother was keen to help and got on his phone to make a couple of calls. He knew some of the key players in Tooting and got one of Crow's olders to locate the phone and have it ready to be picked up, which they managed to do within the hour. Justin, Anton and his older brother that went by the street name Sleepy got in a cab that Sleepy paid for and made their way to pick up the phone. On arrival, they found a group of the Tooting boys including Crow stationed there and Justin felt a real sense of significance as Sleepy let Crow's olders know that his little brother and his friends should be left alone.

Justin went home feeling like a different person. He gave his brother back his phone and, although he told Martin how he'd got it back, Justin lied to his mum, telling her that it had been handed into the school by the police. His mum was over the moon and for a split second he felt like the man of the house.

The rest of the school year was more enjoyable for Justin and his friends: they had some footing in the underground hierarchy and were getting a lot more attention from the girls as word had spread that they associated with a big Brixton gang.

By Year 9 they were established in their school and hailed as the youngers of a notorious Brixton street gang. Justin had been given the street name of Mad Boy by Anton's older brother and Anton went by the name Slinger for short. They would constantly get into fights, and Justin got arrested with a knife on him and had to do community service for four months, narrowly escaping incarceration.

By the time he was fifteen, Justin's mum was aware of the activities he was taking part in, as he had been arrested and neighbours had seen him with groups of youths loitering and smoking weed on the estate, but whenever she tried to talk to him about it he would deny it completely. Justin's younger brother remained neutral and never got involved in the gang life, but on the odd occasion Justin would ask him to hide things, such as offensive weapons and drugs.

Justin felt as if he had big shoes to fill: his older was recognized for being a loose cannon and Justin felt as if he wasn't doing enough. So he vowed in his heart that whenever he got into an altercation he would stab his opponent, so that word would spread round and he would be respected.

Justin saw his father rarely, but whenever his dad did come round the house Justin didn't feel anxiety like before: his dad could no longer hit his mum because he wouldn't stand for it – he was taller than his dad and knew that he could inflict harm if need be.

Justin felt a shift within himself and saw that he was no longer the person he had been before: he had truly changed, and realized the mask he had put on he now couldn't take off. At any potential threats to him and his friends he would constantly have murderous thoughts. He truly believed that it was kill or be killed.

When Justin was sixteen, one of his friends from his gang was murdered by a rival gang member after receiving a stab to the heart at a funfair in Brockwell Park. His friend was also sixteen, but this wasn't a wake-up call for Justin: he automatically put his friend's death down to the fact that him and his team hadn't been thorough enough. His friend was buried seven weeks after his actual death (for six weeks the police had his body for forensics) and his family wasn't able to have an open-casket funeral as his body had decomposed so much. But while the body was in the funeral centre Justin went with his deceased friend's family and a few friends to see him. He was on a table behind a glass, and there Justin saw his light-skinned black friend as coal-black due to the rotting.

Justin cried for two straight days after his friend's death, but had given up on the concept of crying by the time of the funeral. All he could think about was revenge. The newspaper articles around his friend's death had centred on the theme of 'Gangster stabbed dead at Fun Fair'. It truly sank in after all the headlines that this was exactly what he was: a gangster.

The death of Justin's friend caused him to binge on weed and he went from smoking weed three or so times a day to eight or nine times a day. This increase of smoking correlated with an increase of paranoia. Justin felt as if everybody wanted him dead; he even began to have thoughts that some of his gang members' loyalty was questionable. He felt so vulnerable without a firearm, but whenever he had one on his person he felt indestructible.

Justin and his mum were constantly in arguments and one day he struck his brother during an altercation. His mum had enough and kicked him out. He went to apply for a hostel but didn't get one straight away and began staying with one of his punters, an eighteen-year-old single mother living in a hostel not too far from his house. He would give her weed in exchange for sexual favours. They lived together for close to a year and she would aid him by holding drugs and guns for him.

Anton got a hostel and he and Justin moved in together. They had both left secondary school with fewer than five GCSEs, not because they weren't able to get more but because their attention and focus hadn't been on education for a long time. Further education didn't even seem like an option for Justin; he was selling drugs and couldn't get his head around the concept of working legitimately and getting paid £7 an hour when he could make £70 selling weed. At seventeen years old Justin was arrested for murder. He had shot the best friend of the guy that had murdered his own friend a year ago. Police intelligence allowed them to locate the firearm and as they had the murder weapon and his clothes with gunpowder on them, they had a case. He was sentenced to nineteen years in prison. There were two gunmen that had been involved in the murder; the other was Anton, but they hadn't found the second firearm discharged at the scene and no matter how much the police tried to bribe Justin to give up his accomplice he didn't. Anton was arrested but they couldn't get anything to stick so he was cleared later in court.

Justin was sent to Huntercombe Prison and there he received three other charges in his first six months; he had a hopelessly bitter attitude and became very violent. His mum visited him rarely; she couldn't bear to see him behind bars. They moved him to another prison further away up North England where he received a lot of racial attacks; it was almost impossible for him to receive visits as the journey was costly and long. Anton came to see him once every three months. After almost three years of being incarcerated he received news in a letter from his brother informing him that Anton had been shot in the back of the head and lived but was now disabled, dumb and blind in one eye. The pain of feeling alone and helpless overwhelmed him: deep depression overtook Justin and he gradually lost his mind and became schizophrenic. He was sectioned and sent to a mental institution at the age of twenty.

Nathan

Children who have been exposed to the toxic combination of violence and neglect, and who potentially have family vulnerabilities related to mental ill health, may go on to feel so overwhelmed that they develop mental illnesses. Schizophrenia and bi-polar disorders are common. With the individual tipping from the point of extreme emotional distress into a loss of a sense of reality, paranoia, delusions and an altered sense of self can take over. Sadly, mental-health provisions in inner-city environments are chronically under-resourced. Young people can end up on psychiatric wards alongside profoundly crazed adults, with minimal nursing, a lack of activities and psychiatrists who are overworked. A lot of good is being done in these institutions by dedicated individuals – however, collectively, the service is shockingly abysmal, failing both the patients and the workers within it.

A large percentage of the mentally ill end up on the streets. They are unable to sustain housing contracts, pay their bills and abide by social decorum. Instead, they can end up either sleeping rough or travelling from one temporary squat to another. Squatting can be a substitute for a family environment. Some people are professional squatters. They create alternative communities and run them well. But in their cohort will be the mentally ill, the addicted and often runaway children. In 2010, the only children's refuge in the country, with nine beds, shut in London due to a lack of funding. Housing and the lack of a safe space to live are the most serious issues facing many vulnerable young people.

Children of the Underground Grow Up

Childhood maltreatment doesn't end with childhood. Its repercussions can shade the lives of grown-ups who, on the face of it, have greater ability to escape abuse. But they engage in a new battle: the dynamics played out where the abuser and the abused child are held in the inner drama of their mind; at times, the adult is propelled back to the moment of being a helpless victim through flashbacks. At other times, the harming behaviour of the abuser is repeated with the adult behaving as a perpetrator of abuse towards the child within themselves. It can be so subtle: cutting your hair to make yourself look ugly, or running until you can't breathe, as if to re-experience the moment you were battered and left exhausted to the point of breathlessness. It can be starving yourself as your mother starved you, leaving you as a toddler to draw pictures of food on a piece of paper and swallowing it, imagining it to be real. It can be seeking violent partners or battling with your boss as if he was your violent step-father. Add to these challenges the often intrinsic lack of self-worth in whose defence you become grandiose, or in whose shadow you avoid social contact. The constant insidious self-critical voice whispers, 'You'll never be good enough, you're not worthy of love, your achievements are not real, tomorrow you'll be hated as you were yesterday.' It's often the lack of hope that becomes the bleakest legacy of childhood maltreatment. How do you work hard, believe in the momentum of achievement when deep down you know that someone with harmful intentions can unravel your tidy accomplishments? Before anyone can take the good away from you, you take it away from yourself. At least in self-sabotage you remain the master of your destiny, always better than being mastered.

At Kids Company, we also offer support to parents who have suffered childhood maltreatment themselves. It is important to do intensive therapeutic work with carers using psychotherapy, art, coaching and practical interventions. The primary aim is to untangle the emotional life of the adult, separating it from the legacy of their childhood maltreatment. Parents can repeat harm unwittingly. In one of my cases a daughter was sexually abused by her father. Her mother did not protect her. When I met the mother I found her to be completely disconnected, almost knowing that her child had been abused and yet denying it; for example, seeing blood in her pre-pubescent child's underpants, but not enquiring why it was there. Her disassociation was so extreme that on many occasions she let into the house the paedophiles who were subsequently abusing her child. In fact, she found one of them naked in the house and accepted his explanation that he was repairing a door.

This mother is driven by two destructive forces simultaneously. One is to deny the harm that has been caused, the other is to drive her daughter into harm's way so that she gets to be as damaged as she is. In that way, the mother protects herself against any potential envy she might experience as a result of having a girl who was not abused.

Most children spend the majority of their first hours, days and months with their mothers, so their attachment to her in particular is crucial. This critical period is extremely important: if the experience of maternal attachment is negative, this sets a pattern that is very difficult to change in someone's life, even if the child has a loving care-giver later on, i.e. after the critical period – hence the sometimes tragic relationships that negatively attached children grow up to have.

Separation anxiety studies have shown that the relationship between young children and their parents is largely shaped by environmental influences rather than innate mechanisms. This is illustrated in observations made in cross-cultural studies, which have shown that the level of anxiety experienced by infants differed across cultures.[38] Young children cry more when they are separated from their mothers when they have spent a lot of time with them, as is often the case in western society; they cry less when little time is spent with their parents as in the Israeli kibbutz where children spend more time with other children of the same age. Early experiences with care-givers gradually give rise to the 'internal working model of social relationships', a system of thoughts, memories, beliefs, expectations, emotions and behaviours about the self and others.[39] This internal model enables the child to understand new types of social interactions; for example, that an infant should be treated differently to an older child, or that interactions with teachers and parents share characteristics. It continues to develop through adulthood, helping the person to cope with friendships, close relationships and parenthood, all of which involve different behaviours and feelings. The interesting thing is that the people and the relationships in the adult's life are a result of the internal model developed in infanthood, during maternal attachment. If a child experiences their care-giver as a source of security and support, they are more likely to develop a positive self-image and expect positive reactions from others. Conversely, a child whose care-giver is abusive may internalize a negative self-image and generalize negative expectations into other relationships. Development often continues in a similar direction and, in the case of negatively attached children, this can create a nasty string of negative relationships.

Children who experience the prolonged absence of their mother, breakdown in communication, emotional unavailability or signs of rejection or abandonment during infanthood grow into insecure young people and adults. When psychologists realized that the effects of attachment continued into adulthood, attachment theory was extended to encompass adult romantic relationships. In the late 1980s four styles of attachment were identified: secure, anxious-preoccupied, dismissive-avoidant and fearful-avoidant.[40]

These roughly correspond to the infant classifications: secure, insecure-ambivalent, insecure-avoidant. According to this theory, securely attached adults tend to have positive views of themselves, their partners and their relationships. They feel comfortable with intimacy and independence, balancing the two. Anxious-preoccupied adults seek high levels of intimacy, approval and responsiveness from partners, becoming overly dependent. They tend to be less trusting, have less positive views about themselves and their partners, and may exhibit high levels of emotional expressiveness, worry and impulsiveness in their relationships.

Dismissive-avoidant adults desire a high level of independence, often appearing to avoid attachment altogether. They view themselves as self-sufficient, invulnerable to attachment feelings and not needing close relationships. They tend to suppress their feelings, dealing with rejection by distancing themselves from partners, of whom they often have a poor opinion. Fearful-avoidant adults have mixed feelings about close relationships, both desiring and feeling uncomfortable with emotional closeness. They tend to mistrust their partners and view themselves as unworthy. Like dismissive-avoidant adults, fearful-avoidant adults tend to seek less intimacy, suppressing their feelings.

Below is the experience of a young adult, who, as well as achieving a degree in experimental psychology at one of the country's leading universities, was also once a homeless girl on the streets. She shares candidly the challenge she continues to face:

I used to have very few successful relationships.
I wanted to be loved but I feared rejection so
much that I did not allow people to become too
close to me. I also expected people to reject and
avoid me, so I often interpreted people's behaviour
as signs that they were doing this. I then behaved
in a way that would guarantee they would reject
me – I thought that if I caused people to reject
me it would hurt much less. I still struggle with
these things; every day I have to weigh up the
facts against my skewed view of what people think
of me and are trying to do to me.

I did not have any evidence that I was loveable
because I sought out people who treated me like
my mother and this further ingrained my feelings
of worthlessness. It was only when I was loved
unconditionally by my keyworker that I started to
have better relationships. Regardless of what I did,
however much I pushed her away, she continued
to care about and check on me; it was surreal.
I did not think it was possible and I definitely did
not think I was worth it. Personally I think my

insecure attachment made me very detached from other people.

Insecure attachment patterns can compromise exploration and the achievement of self-confidence. A securely attached baby is free to concentrate on her or his environment. I have an insecure attachment; I have very little self-confidence and self-worth despite what people tell me and what I have achieved. Objectively I can see I have a lot to be proud of but I still often feel I have achieved nothing useful and there is no point to my life. I have learnt the hard way, on numerous occasions, that objectivity and rationality have nothing to do with emotions and feeling.

Around 65 per cent of children in the general population may be classified as having a secure pattern of attachment, with the remaining 35 per cent being divided between the insecure classifications.[41] Recent research has sought to ascertain the extent to which a parent's attachment classification is predictive of their children's classification. Parents' perceptions of their own childhood attachments were found to predict their children's classifications 75 per cent of the time.[42] My mother had an awful relationship with her mother and our relationship is non-existent; I can only pray that because I am aware of the problem and have taken steps to improve my emotional development the vicious cycle will stop with me.

A child's behaviour when reunited with a care-giver is determined not only by how the care-giver has treated the child before, but on the history of effects the child has had on the care-giver.[43] Many children are not planned and many people have children for the wrong selfish reasons. My mother told me she had me to improve the relationship between herself and my father. She also explained her disappointment that I was a girl because Nigerian men like boys; this is why my brother and I are so close in age. Once again, a vicious cycle resulting in a broken relationship that is near impossible to fix.

Insecure attachment causes many direct problems; however these go on to cause more problems. I often felt that there was part of me missing, a part of me that could not be filled by what I was trying to fill it with: sex, money, material things, drugs, etc. This lack of fulfilment led to me thinking a baby would fill this hole and I came extremely close to getting my wish. Other women who felt the same as me got their wish and realized the hard way that it would make no difference. It probably also continues the cycle of insecure attachment, as the mother's feelings towards the child could be of disappointment that the child is not fulfilling its purpose.

There is light at the end of the tunnel: due to the plasticity of the brain, providing a secure maternal attachment outside the critical period in childhood can have significant positive effects. Also, therapy, which retrains the adult's way of interacting with others and thinking about those interactions, can be useful. I have had both and words cannot describe the positive effects they have had on my life. I wouldn't be where I am today if it wasn't for Kids Company. They provided me with someone

I could become securely attached to; this taught me how to have positive relationships with other people and how to manage my own emotions. Neither are perfect but they are much better than they used to be.

The Final Stop

Together with some incredibly courageous and dignified young people, we have tried to make underground childhoods visible. No one can promise to eliminate child abuse, but we can provide better protection and intervention for children who have been catastrophically harmed. It's about first being able to imagine their pain, and then having enough passion to provide a framework of lifelong support.

Individuals who receive early and robust therapeutic interventions are less likely to recycle their childhood maltreatment, and to harm others in the process. I hope, from the narratives shared, that we take on board the messages from the children about the potency of attachment and loving care. If a biological carer fails to deliver, despite the fact that their position is unique and irreplaceable, there is no reason why compassionate strangers can't step in to protect and re-parent a child who has been harmed. Some children can be looked after in foster families, others are too disturbed and will require more professional home settings. A group will thrive and flourish if there is access to a protective and caring environment at street level on a daily basis.

What all these children are looking for is a kind and nurturing substitute family experience with adults who have a passion for their wellbeing and who can help each child develop personal strategies for managing the legacy of childhood maltreatment.

It's not clinical settings, doctors in white coats, therapists vanilla'd by neutrality that these children need; they want a home from home where the parental figures are good enough to protect them, inspiring enough to motivate them and consistent enough to withstand the vicissitudes of their recovery.

Over the last sixteen years, the children of Kids Company, its staff and its supporters have endeavoured to grow a substitute re-parenting community. It is under-resourced, still learning from its mistakes, but the foundations are strengthened every day by the integrity of being able to work through love.

We have a dream that one day our politicians will have enough moral courage to stand up for vulnerable children, despite the fact that from them they can gain no vote. We have a vision that the voting public will embrace the children's needs and hold the politicians accountable for their wellbeing. Children who have been harmed carry an unfair burden; as the rest of us travel through our daily lives, they contemplate ending theirs because the loneliness, the abandonment, the being discarded becomes too unbearable.

Fly

I just had the most incredible urge to throw myself
    off the balcony
To fly for my last few moments on Earth
To be free from the prison that is my mind
My thoughts
My feelings
To end it all
I recognize this feeling
It is sometimes there when I see train tracks

Surely we have the power to change this girl's journey and the journey of other children like her. Compassion is the ticket.

Notes

1. 'Seen and Now Heard: Taking action on child neglect', Action for Children, 2010.
2. 'Child poverty in perspective: An overview of child well-being in rich countries', Innocenti Report Card 7, 2007.
3. The figures quoted are from the following sources:
4. 2008: http://www.prisonreformtrust.org.uk/ Portals/0/Documents/criminal%20damge%- 20-%20why%20we%20should%20lock%20 up%20fewer%20children.pdf
5. 2008: http://www.guardian.co.uk/society/ 2008/apr/02/prisonsandprobation.housing

6. 1997: http://www.youngminds.org.uk/training _services/policy/mental_health_statistics

7. 1999: http://www.guardian.co.uk/news/ datablog/2009/sep/11/child-poverty-statistics-uk-countries

8. 2004: http://www.avaproject.org.uk/ our-resources/statistics/prostitution.aspx

9. 2011: http://makerunawayssafe.org.uk/sites/ default/files/Still-Running-3_Full-Report_ FINAL.pdf

10. 2010-2011: http://www.education.gov.uk/ researchandstatistics/statistics/allstatistics/ a00199334/children-in-need-in-england-2010-11

11. 2010: http://www.nhstayside.scot.nhs.uk/ Suicide/Suicide%20-%20final%20copy.pdf

12. 2010: http://www.libdemvoice.org/the-independent-view-child-abuse-cuts-and-peace-of-mind-for-kids-20249.html

13. http://www.thesun.co.uk/sol/homepage/ news/4133228/Million-youngsters-bear-brunt-of-unemployment.html

14. Data gathered in external and internal evaluations, Kids Company, 2008–2012.

15. Home Office and Ministry of Justice, 'Statistical Bulletin on the public disorder of 6–9 August 2011.'

16. Price, D. et al, *Building Brains: An Introduction to Neural Development*, 2011.

17. Center on the Developing Child, Harvard University, 'The Timing and Quality of Early Experiences Combine to Shape Brain Architecture', 2007. http://developingchild.net/pubs/wp-abstracts/wp5.html

18. Lebel, C., and Beaulieu, C., 'Longitudinal development of human brain wiring continues from childhood into adulthood,' *The Journal of Neuroscience*, 31 (30), 10937–47 PMID: 21795544, 2011.

19. McCrory et al, 'Heightened neural reactivity to threat in child victims of family violence' *Current Biology*, Vol. 21, Issue 23, pp. R947–R948, 2011.

20. Mueller, S. C., Maheu, F. S., Dozier, M., Peloso, E., Mandell, D., Leibenluft, E., Pinea, D. S., and Ernsta, M.,'Early-life stress is associated with impairment in cognitive control in adolescence:

an fMRI study.' *Neuropsychologia* 48, 3037–3044, 2010.

21. Center on the Developing Child at Harvard University, 'Excessive stress disrupts the architecture of the developing brain,' Working Paper No. 3. http://www.developingchild. net/pubs/wp/Stress_Disrupts_Architecture_ Developing_Brain.pdf., 2005.

22. Sotres-Bayon, F., Bush, D. E., LeDoux, J. E., *Neurobiology of Learning and Memory*, 11, 525 (2004).

23. Shonkoff, J. P., and Phillips, D. (Eds.), 'From Neurons to Neighborhoods: The science of early childhood development,' Committee on Integrating the Science of Early Childhood Development, Washington, DC: National Academy Press, 2000.

24. Perry, B. D. and Pollard, D., 'Altered brain development following global neglect in early childhood,' Society for Neuroscience: Proceedings from Annual Meeting, New Orleans, 1997.

25. Karmarkar, U. R. and Dan, Y., 'Experience-dependent plasticity in adult visual cortex,' *Neuron*, 52, 577–585, 2006.

26. Huttenlocher, P. R., 'Neural plasticity: The effects of environment on the development of the cerebral cortex,' Cambridge, MA: Harvard University Press, 2002.

27. Blakemore, S.-J., and Choudhury, S., 'Development of the adolescent brain: implications for executive function and social cognition', *Journal of Child Psychology and Psychiatry*, 47, 296–312, 2006.

28. Murphy, Timothy H. and Corbett, Dale, 'Plasticity during stroke recovery: from synapse to behaviour,' *Nature Reviews Neuroscience* 10, 861-872 doi:10.1038/nrn2735 (2009).

29. Hart, H., Rubia, K., 'Neuroimaging of child abuse: A critical review', *Frontiers in Human Neuroscience* 19 March 2012 doi: 10.3389/fnhum.2012.00052

30. Pears, K. C., Kim, H. K., and Fisher, P. A., 'Psychosocial and cognitive functioning of

children with specific profiles of maltreatment,' *Child Abuse & Neglect*, 32(10), 958–971, 2008.

31. Mueller, S., Maheu, F., Dozier, M., Peloso, E., Mandell, D., Leibenluft, E., and Ernsta, M., 'Early-life stress is associated with impairment in cognitive control in adolescence: an fMRI study,' *Neuropsychologia*, 48(10), 3037–3044, 2010.

32. Lupien, S. J., DeLeon, M., DeSanti, S., Convit, A., Tarshish, C., Nair, N. P. V., Thakur, M., McEwen, B. S., Hauger, R. L., Meaney, M. J., 1998. 'Longitudinal increase in cortisol during human aging predicts hippocampal atrophy and memory deficits,' *Nature Neuroscience* 1, 69–73.

33. Lanius, R. A., Williamson, P. C., Densmore, M., Boksman, K., Gupta, M. A., Neufeld, R. W., Gati, J. S., and Menon, R. S., 'Neural correlates of traumatic memories in posttraumatic stress disorder: a functional MRI investigation,' *American Journal of Psychiatry* 158, 1920–1922, 2001.

34. Edmiston, E., Wang, F., Mazure, C., Guiney, J., Sinha, R., Mayes, L., and Blumberg, H., 'Corticostriatal-limbic gray matter morphology

in adolescents with self-reported exposure to childhood maltreatment,' Archives of *Pediatric and Adolescent Medicine*, 165(12), 1069–1077, 2011.

35. De Bellis et al, *Biological Psychiatry* 1999; 45:1271–1284.

36. Shin, L. M., Rauch, S. L., and Pitman, R. K. (2006). 'Amygdala, medial prefrontal cortex, and hippocampal function in PTSD,' Annals of the New York Academy of Sciences, 1071, 67–79, 2006.

37. McCrory. Eamon J., et al, 'Heightened neural reactivity to threat in child victims of family violence,' *Current biology*, volume 21, issue 23 pp. R947–R948, 2011.

38. Van Ijzendoorn, M. and Kroonenberg, P., 'Cross-Cultural Patterns of Attachment: A Meta-Analysis of the Strange Situation,' *Child Development*, Vol. 59, No. 1 pp. 147–156, 1988.

39. Mercer, J. *Understanding Attachment: Parenting, Child Care and Emotional Development*, Greenwood Press, 2005.

40. Hazan, C. & Shaver, P., 'Romantic Love conceptualized as an attachment process,'

Journal of Personality and Social Psychology, 52(3), 511–524, 1987.

41. Prior, V. and Glaser, D. *Understanding attachment and attachment disorders: Theory, evidence and practice*, Jessica Kingsley Pub, 2006.

42. Fonagy, P., Steele, H., and Steele, M.,'Maternal representations of attachment during pregnancy predict the organization of infant-mother attachment at one year of age,' *Child Development*, 62(5), 891–905, 1991.

43. Ainsworth, M. D. S., 'Object relations, dependency, and attachment: A theoretical review of the infant-mother relationship,' *Child Development*, 969–1025, 1969.

PENGUIN LINES
Choose Your Journey

If you're looking for...

Romantic Encounters

Heads and Straights
by Lucy Wadham
(the Circle line)

Waterloo–City, City–Waterloo
by Leanne Shapton
(the Waterloo & City line)

Tales of Growing Up and Moving On

Heads and Straights
by Lucy Wadham
(the Circle line)

A Good Parcel of English Soil
by Richard Mabey
(the Metropolitan line)

Mind the Child
by Camila Batmanghelidjh and
Kids Company
(the Victoria line)

The 32 Stops
by Danny Dorling
(the Central line)

*A History of Capitalism
According to the Jubilee Line*
by John O'Farrell
(the Jubilee line)

A Northern Line Minute
by William Leith
(the Northern line)

Mind the Child
by Camila Batmanghelidjh and
Kids Company
(the Victoria line)

Heads and Straights
by Lucy Wadham
(the Circle line)

Laughter and Tears

Breaking Boundaries

Drift
by Philippe Parreno
(the Hammersmith & City line)

Buttoned-Up
by Fantastic Man
(the East London line)

Waterloo–City, City–Waterloo
by Leanne Shapton
(the Waterloo & City line)

Earthbound
by Paul Morley
(the Bakerloo line)